MAMMOTH - MONO COUNTRY

Lundy Canyon

Mono Lake

Minarets Wilderness

June Lake
Loop

Mammoth
Lakes

Crowley Lake

Devils Postpile

Convict Lake

Hwy. 395

Rock Creek

MAMMOTH - MONO COUNTRY

Lew & Ginny Clark

©Lewis D. Clark & Virginia D. Clark, 1981
All rights reserved
ISBN 0-931532-17-5
Western Trails Publications
P.O. Box 1697
San Luis Obispo, Ca, 93406

MOUNTAIN BREEZE

I wish I were a mountain breeze
    That wanders on o'er hill and dale
    Sighing softly through stalwart trees
    And caressing flowers in mountain vale.

I'd wander up the canyon walls
    Where cliff swallows dart and sway,
    Then pause to listen in wooded halls
    Where warblers sing and chickarees play.

I'd drift along the river's breast
    Capturing the fragrance of azalia bowers
    And drifting on o'er waterfall's crest
    Gather mists for summer showers.

Then, once again I'd sweep the crests
    Along skyline's glacial cirques, and
    There in quiet contentment rest
    In wonderment at our Creator's works.

—Lewis W. Clark
1904–1979

TABLE OF CONTENTS

MAMMOTH ~ MONO COUNTRY

The maps with trails and elevation contours guide you through this region. With these enlarged photographs on the preceding and next pages taken by the U.S. Air Force some 65,000' up, the land becomes more visual.

You can imagine the extent of the glaciers that once covered the area and understand how the rivers and lakes were formed more clearly. For instance, looking at Duck Lake on the preceding page, when the glacier receded, Duck and Pika lakes were held in by the moraine dam and is now enclosed by higher peaks to rest in its own basin. Little Pika Lake was formed by a smaller moraine which separated the bodies of water to make two instead of one large lake.

It is fantastic to see just how numerous the lakes are in these mountains. Notice the steep-wall trench of the North Fork of the San Joaquin River between the Ritter Range and boundary crest of Yosemite National Park. Or, how the main San Joaquin River between the Ritter Range and the Mammoth-San Joaquin Range flows south cutting through below the Ritter Range before turning westward to the Pacific Ocean. This major river's headwaters are EAST of the Sierra Crest.

Contrasts are evident in environments; the Mammoth Lakes are enclosed with an evergreen forest while Convict Lake is open and exposed. The many

MAMMOTH COUNTRY

east Sierra canyons are made of lateral moraines as Lundy, Laurel, LeeVining and McGee. Mono Craters are more appealing here than on flat maps and the size of Mono Lake is more appalling.

This Mammoth-Mono Country is rich in variety, with scenic adventures in desert, forest, mountain, and alpine environments. The mountainous regions receive the greatest rainfall and snowfall while the lowest slopes and valleys are arid and the air is dry. Most of the precipitation occurs between November and March with the greatest amount of snowfall above 8000'. The amount of snowfall, the exposure, and proximity of both Mammoth and June Mountains to an open, major highway allows this country to be a viable year round recreational area.

Because of the climatic conditions and elevation differences, vegetation is as various as the landscape—ranging from bitterbrush, sagebrush and pinyon pine in the high desert; jeffrey pines that grow in the Transition Life Zone; the Canadian Life Zone of the white and red firs and lodgepole pines; the hardy mountain hemlock of the Hudsonian Life Zone; to the gnarly whitebark pines of the Alpine Life Zone. Flowers are abundant with many varieties in all zones.

More than 150 birds, 75 mammals, and 15 reptiles and amphibian species may be seen. Deer, bear and coyote are prevelant, with squirrels, chipmunks, pine martens, woodpeckers, chickadees, and nuthatches. Marmots and rosy finches inhabit the rugged climate near and above the timberline.

MONO COUNTRY

MAMMOTH LAKES

The glint of sunlight on the yellow gold or blue-gray silver taken from the Mammoth Mine in the late 1800's were never to match the rewards of its white, snowy peaks, sky-blue lakes, and deep green forests.

Prospectors came to the Mammoth region to locate the "Lost Cement Mine"—where gold nuggets resembled large "raisins in a pudding." Enough gold and silver was found here to start a rush in 1877. A toll-trail was built from Fresno Flats (now called Oakhurst) to bring in supplies from the San Joaquin Valley. Part of this route is known as the French or Old Mammoth Trail extending between Clover Meadows and Mammoth Lakes (see map page 32).

The new camp developed rapidly. Much of the production was from the Mammoth Mine which yielded $200,000 between 1878-1881. A mining district was formed in 1887. By then several thousand people lived in the make-shift "cities" of Mammoth City, Mill City and Pine City. As elsewhere, the returns soon began to fade. Some mining was done in the late 1890's and early 1900's. Other spurts of activity took place in the 1930's and some in the 1950's.

The principal mines were: Argosy, Beauregard — $1,000,000; Don Quixote, Lisbon, Mammoth — $200,000; Mammoth Consolidated — $100,000; Monte Cristo — $100,000, and the Sierra Group. It became evident that the total development and operation costs on these mines exceeded their total return.

Todays visitors will find only the remains of a few log cabins, pieces of rusty machinery scattered among the grass, and great piles of rock near diggings resembling abandoned coyote holes.

As ranching became more stabilized in the Owens Valley, people began to enjoy camping out in the cool forested area of Mammoth Lakes. Between 1920 and 1930 tent cabins were built at Lake Mary, Lake Mamie, and Twin Lakes to accommodate paying guests and visitors from the "outside." Eventually the fishing, hunting, and family camping became the major industry preluding the success of the community today.

In 1938 the new township of Mammoth Lakes was established. Dave McCoy set up the first rope-tow on Mammoth Mountain and ski races were established by winter sports groups. Permanent buildings were erected to house the year round activities. Campgrounds were established by the Forest Service.

A vast survey is being conducted by the Forest Service for the entire Mammoth-Mono Country to prepare for the future recreational facilities necessary for its expected millions of visitors per year to this area.

In Mammoth Lakes are six churches of various faiths, hospital, Mono County Medical Health Clinic, Library, and all modern services. The Summer Music Festival; the Fourth of July Gold Rush Days with parade and other gaities; the Mammoth Lakes International Arts and Crafts Festival; the annual MotoCross race and Tennis Tournament all measure the cultural spirit of the present mountain city. Public tennis courts are on the Forest Trail Road. The MotoCross course is on the Sherwin Road.

Mammoth Lakes Basin

Trails around and between the Lakes in the forested basin are especially rewarding for day walks or evening strolls among the pines or along the lakeshore. The trails are not too steep but pleasant with little climbs. Flowers are prevelant in the meadows and the pines and hemlocks shelter the wildlife that live there.

TWIN LAKES: 8540'. 30 acres. Good fishing for Rainbow, Eastern Brook and Brown trout. Store. Boat rentals. NO motors. Handicap pier. Foot bridge separate lakes. Forest Chapel. Scenic Twin Falls with picnic area. Tamarack Lodge. 96 campsites.

LAKE MARY: 8931'. 140 acres. Good fishing for Rainbow, Eastern Brook and Brown trout. Store. Boat rentals. Yes on motors at 10 mph max. Pokonobe Lodge. Crystal Crag Lodge. 50 campsites at Lake Mary CG; 12 campsites at Pine City CG; 78 campsites at Coldwater Creek CG. Wilderness Trailhead.

LAKE MAMIE: 8898'. 19 acres. Good fishing for Rainbow, Eastern Brook, and Brown trout. Boat rentals. Yes on motors at 10 mph max. Wildyrie Lodge and Store.

LAKE GEORGE: 9008'. 38 acres. Good fishing for Rainbow, Eastern Brook, Brown trout. Boat rentals. Yes on motors at 10 mph max. Store. Woods Lodge. 37 campsites. Wilderness Trailhead.

LAKES BARRET and T.J.: NO boats, motors or facilities. Hike in from Lake George.

CRYSTAL LAKE: 9250'. Moderate 1.4 mi. from Lake George. Good fishing for Rainbow, Eastern Brook and Brown trout. No facilities.

HORSESHOE LAKE: 8950'. 53 acres. Good fishing for Rainbow and Brown Trout. Boating. NO motors. No store. Swimming on sandy beach area. Group camping only — 385 sites. Reservations necessary. Picnic area. Wilderness Trailhead.

McCLOUD LAKE: No boats, motors or facilities. 1.5 miles from Horseshoe Lake.

15

MAMMOTH LAKES   ROCKY ROCKWELL

TWIN LAKES   L. DEAN CLARK

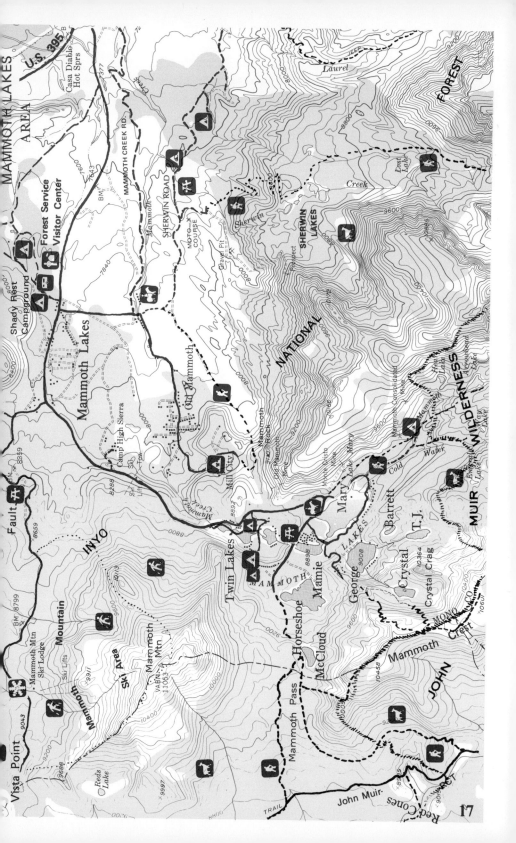

JUNE LAKE

Long before the arrival of prospectors and white settlers came to explore and live in this country, the Paiute Indians found Reversed Creek Canyon and its lakes an excellent homeland. There are numerous remains of their old campsites. The forest provided good shelter and fuel for their fires. The desert shrub-covered hills to the east were full of game and the bubbling streams among the aspens were full of fish. They traded obsidian found down in Deadman Creek for acorns from the Miwok Indians of Yosemite. The meeting place was near Mono Pass, which later became a principal west-east pack route across the Sierra.

Approaching the Loop from the south for the first time, the incline from June Lake Junction to the Oh! Ridge does not prepare the visitor for the magnificent westward panorama at the summit. A lookout, geology display and parking area is to the right just below the summit. Stop and take pictures and enjoy this spectacular mountain scene of high rugged peaks, shimmering blue lakes, and a community nestled in the valley below.

The beauty of June Lake is not seasonal. Each time of the year special mountain landscapes inspire visitors — spring wildflowers and full-bodied creeks gurgling with icy run-offs; lazy summer breeze with aspens quivering along the lake shores, the brilliant yellow, gold and orange leaves mixed with the dark green pines against the gray granite hillsides at autumn, and the chilling beauty of winter with snow-covered mountain peaks.

The U.S. Forest Service has established campsites and rest areas for the visitor. In 1960 they granted a lease to build the June Mountain Ski Lift. Since then additional ski and winter resort facilities have provided a great year round resort with both summer and winter sports.

JUNE LAKE LOOP

Originally this area was called Horseshoe Canyon. It was so named by the surveyor for the government, because the flow of the lakes and streams at the base of this mountain formation was unusual. Visitors have been puzzled by the fact that June and Gull lakes and Reversed Creek flow west toward the Sierra instead of away from them to the east.

As geologists explain it, the Rush Creek glacier and other tributary ice flows from the Koip Peak crest cut deeper into the valley northward along the Rush Creek course to Mono Lake. The much harder bedrock of the Oh! Ridge moraine closed off that eastward exit as the glacier receded. It was a large glacier covering the entire Rush Creek basin westward to the Mt. Dana-Koip Crest's eastward slope. There are several small existing glaciers around Koip Peak, on the east side below Parker Peak and on the west slope below Kuna Point.

When the glacier melted leaving June and Gull lakes dammed from the moraines, rocks and boulders which has been picked up along the way and dragged here, were also left. By the road one such huge boulder is seen perched on top of another huge boulder. These are called erratic. Other geologic evidences can be seen on the granite domes between June and Gull lakes. They were shaped by the granite intrusions which formed most of the Sierra. On them you can see glacial scours, glacial polish and other erratic boulders.

Grant Lake terminates Rush Creek. It is a reservoir—a man-made lake built by Los Angeles Department of Water and Power. The desert-like quality of the landscape surrounding this clear open waters is in direct contrast to the aspen-shored Silver Lake. A new overnight Rest Area for RV's has been constructed by the U.S. Forest Service below Grant Lake at Aerie Crag.

For large groups wishing to camp in the June Lake Loop, a campground near Fern Creek is reserved for Boy Scouts, Church Groups, and youth associations.

June Lake Village is a complete shopping center. In the Alpine setting there are supermarkets, sporting goods stores, gift shops, laundromat, restaurants, service stations, and garages. Everything needed for a great vacation can be found here.

Frontier Pack Train out of June Lake makes backcountry trips into the Hoover and Minaret Wilderness areas. P.O. Box 123, June Lake, CA, 93529.

There are many lodges and motels operating in the winter as well as summer. For a complete list contact the June Lake Chamber of Commerce for all available services.

TRAILER PARKS

On the north side of June Lake west of Oh! Ridge summit the Pine Cliff Resort and Trailer Park offers supplies in the general store, trailer rentals and storage as well as modern trailer spaces, laundry and showers.

Silver Lake Resort has a trailer park, cafe, store, boat and motor rentals, housekeeping cabins and fishing supplies.

The Grant Lake Marina has trailer accommodations, dumping station, showers, cafe, store and marine with boat and motor rentals.

At Fern Creek Lodge is a grocery and sporting goods store with modern **19** housekeeping cabins but no camping or trailer facilities.

RUSH CREEK FALLS   L. DEAN CLARK

AROUND JUNE LAKE

Fishing is one of the most favorite summer sports. The many bait and tackle shops in town will assist you in the correct lure to use and places to fish to the best advantage. The continuous heavy planting of trout throughout the season keeps up with the demand even though natural production is considerable. The species of trout planted are Eastern Brook, Rainbow, and Cutthroat. In Grant Lake and along Rush Creek some Brown Trout can be found. All types of fishing are possible: trolling in the lake, spin-fishing with cow bells, fly fishing, or just bait worms, cheese, eggs and hook.

For the equestrian visit the Pack Station near Silver Lake for hourly, day or more extensive backcountry trips into the higher more primitive areas.

For hikers, there are several good day trips:

INDIAN ROCK, which lies at the west end of Gull Lake, affords a great view of the southern half of the June Lake Loop.

FERN LAKE and YOST LAKE can be reached by the Fern Creek Trail. To reach Yost Lake, when the trail reaches Fern Creek, cross and head toward Yost Creek climbing up to the Lake. For Fern Lake climb south along Fern Creek to the lake.

REVERSED PEAK TRAIL is NO longer maintained and it is a dangerous, very strenuous climb. Forest Service Rangers can point out the best cross-country route.

AGNEW LAKE Trail starts at Silver Lake. It is a 2.0 mile hike up 1300 ft. start early in the morning before the sun beats down and makes the climb through the exposed sagebrush slope uncomfortably warm. Take your lunch and enjoy a picnic at the lake. There is a table and small campsite for overnighters going further into the backcountry.

PARKER LAKE can be reached via the old jeep road from the south near Silver Lake or north of Grant Lake starting at the trail junction near the aquaduct.

20 GOOD NEWS FOR CYCLISTS: A new bicycle trail is planned to be made by the Forest Service to go around the June Lake Loop.

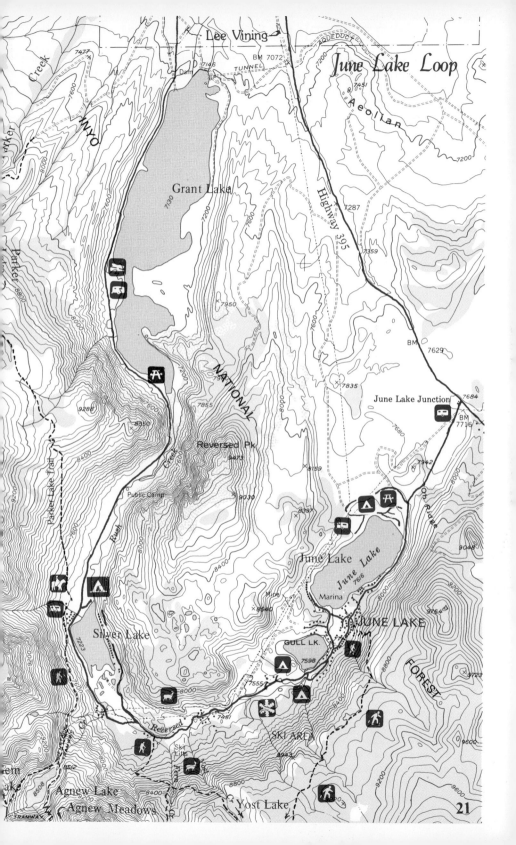

Lee Vining

Creek

7477

BM 7072

Dam 7145 TUNNEL

AQUEDUCT

Aeolian

7451

7200

INYO

7600

8000

Grant Lake

7130

7200

7287

Highway 395

7359

7950

7600

7600

BM
7629

7835

June Lake Junction

7684

9288

NATIONAL

7855

BM
7716

7680

7942

Reversed Pk
9475

Creek

8159

Ott Ridge

8000

Parker Lake Trail

8400

Public Camp

9030

3357

9048

Bush Creek

8400

June Lake

June Lake

761.6

9200

Silver Lake

7223

Mine
9540

Marina

JUNE LAKE

9264.9

FOREST

GULL LK.

7598

9723

Reversed

7451

7555

8000

8800

SKI AREA

4943

Ski Lifts

9600

8512

8808

Agnew Lake
Agnew Meadows

8400

8800

Yost Lake

9600

TRAMWAY

21

DEVILS POSTPILE — REDS MEADOW

The introduction of the shuttle bus system down to the floor of the San Joaquin River Valley to Agnew Meadows, Devils Postpile and Red's Meadow gives the visitor an opportunity to look around at the country instead of the road. Descending on the west slope of the San Joaquin Ridge through a forest, the pumice base of this valley floor is not evident until past the turn at the Agnes Meadows junction.

There are many campgrounds along the river — one at Agnew Meadows, four in the Inyo National Forest Area, one group campground near the Forest Service Ranger Station, and one campground at Devils Postpile National Monument. Picnic sites are at Starkweather and Sotcher lakes. The Hot Springs at the Red's Meadow campground are open to the public, a most refreshing shower after a hot day on the dusty trail.

Ranger programs are at Devils Postpile Campground. Fishing is good along the river or at the lakes. Boats are permitted on Sotcher Lake but no motors.

Red's Meadow Resort and Pack Station has cabins, restaurant, soda fountain, gasoline, groceries, fishing tackle, and a pack station. This is the shuttle bus terminal area for hikers to Rainbow Falls.

Bob Tanner operates both the Red's Meadow and Agnew Meadow Pack Station. Daily rides can be made to Rainbow Falls, and through the Devils Postpile and Agnew Meadow area. His backcountry territory covers Fish Valley to Silver Divide, Mammoth Crest, over Summit Pass to the south, and Shadow, Thousand Island Lakes and Waugh Lake to the north. Box 395, Mammoth Lakes, CA, 93546.

RAINBOW FALLS   L. DEAN CLARK

This beautiful flow of the San Joaquin River over the lava ledge is particularly colorful in the afternoon when the sun creates a rainbow mist. There are several excellent photographic points from the top and front. There is a steep, but short trail down to the base of the falls. The mist from the falls could soak you. The many flowers and trees at the base are very appealing in their refreshing cool air environment.

22

The pumice and crumbly granite fragments at the edges along the gorge are extremely precipitous. Extreme care of footing is necessary.

The formation of the Devils Postpile is of volcanic origin and had its beginnings in the great earthquake fault that lies along the east side of the Sierra range. Weaknesses along this fracture allowed great flows of lava to pour forth, some to 1,000' in depth.

As these flows cooled off, their uniformity of material and temperature caused an evenness of stress on the surface of the shrinking lava. Cracks, in geometric patterns, developed in much the same way as they do in mud flats when they dry up. These cracks joined together, forming four to seven sided units 20'' to 30'' in diameter. As the cooling process continued, the cracking changed from horizontal action on the surface to vertical action downward to the base of the flow, forming huge columns or ''posts.''

In subsequent geologic eras the glaciers passed over this region, cutting down the thickness of the lava flows, and tore away whole sections, leaving exposed the sheer columns of basalt. The evidences of this glacial action are still seen in the great pile of posts below the formation and the polished surface of the tops of many sections still standing.

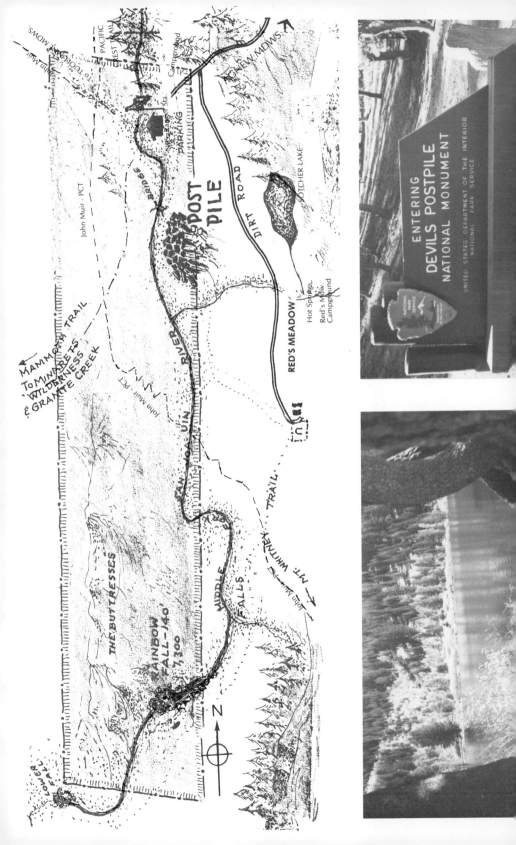

MINARETS WILDERNESS TRAILS

Leading Into Yosemite National Park

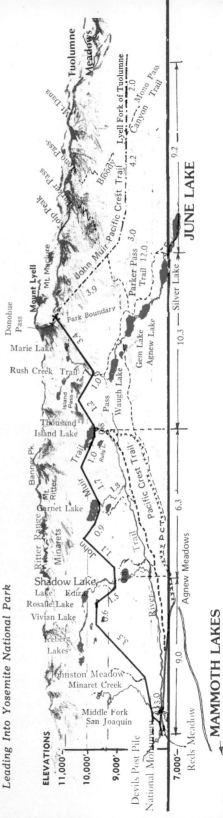

Tuolumne Meadows

Mt. Dana

Lyell Fork of Tuolumne

Mono Pass

Canyon Trail

2.0

Mono Pass

Koip Peak

Parker Pass

Kuna Crest Pass

John Muir–Pacific Crest Trail

Broody

4.2

JUNE LAKE

Mount Lyell

Mt. MacClure

Parker Pass Trail 12.0.

3.0

9.2

Donohue Pass

Park Boundary

3.9

Silver Lake

Marie Lake

Gem Lake

Agnew Lake

Rush Creek Trail

3.4

1.0

10.3

Island Pass

Waugh Lake

Thousand Island Lake

1.2

Pass

0.8

Banner Pk.

1.0

Ruby L.

Pacific Crest Trail

Mt. Ritter

Muir

1.7

Ritter Range

Garnet Lake

1.8

Minarets

6.3

John

0.9

Trail

Agnew Meadows

Shadow Lake

1.1

Lake Ediza

0.8

Rosalie Lake

Trail

Vivian Lake

PCT

Iceberg Lakes

4.5

0.6

River

9.0

Johnston Meadow

3.5

Minaret Creek

MAMMOTH LAKES

Middle Fork San Joaquin

3.0

Reds Meadow

Devils Post Pile National Monument

ELEVATIONS

11,000'

10,000'

9,000'

7,000'

25

MINARET WILDERNESS

TOM JOHNSTON.

This is THE country. It is not hard to understand why when looking at the topo map; the large impressive Thousand Island and Garnet lakes; the Banner Peak, Mt. Ritter, and the entire escarpment of the Bitter Range; the glaciers on the east face of the crest; the many lakes in cirques and moraine basins, the streams and waterfalls, and the trails that lead the traveler through this mountain wonderland.

Many short or more extensive backpacking trips can be planned to the lakes to fish or visit. The John Muir Trail is high and goes along 1000 Island, Garnet, and many other lakes. The River Trail is lower in elevation and follows the San Joaquin River. The Pacific Crest Trail is east of the river, higher up on the bench with views of the deep canyon below and the Ritter Range to the west.

Trails lead from Devils Postpile, Agnew Meadows or June Lake to Yosemite National Park over Donohue Pass, beyond Island Pass. Many side trips can be taken from the John Muir Trail. One of the most popular is going up Shadow Creek, around and over Volcanic Ridge to Minaret Lake and down Minaret Creek to Johnston Meadow joining the John Muir Trail to Devils Postpile.

Nydiver Lake turnoff is about one mile up Shadow Creek from the John Muir Trail. A good cross-country route can be made via switchbacks to these three lakes where the views eastward to the Owens Valley are most impressive.

From Ediza, Iceberg, and Cecile lakes the rugged east face of Mt. Ritter and Banner Peak and the jagged Minarets are overwhelming. Mountain climbers find that meadows around these lakes make good base camps. There is no firewood for cooking in these high exposed, windy alpine shores. On the Ediza-Minaret Lake cross-country the route largely depends on the amount of snow and runoff.

26   The peaks in the Ritter Range are a real challenge to mountain climbers. Remember, however, they should not be attempted alone or by amateur climbers.

Emerald Lake

A very popular two-day circle trip can be made from Agnew Meadows hiking through this great Minarets Wilderness. Starting at either the River Trail or the Pacific Coast Trail go north to Thousand Island Lake to meet the John Muir Trail. Or, for a shorter trip to the John Muir Trail take the Garnet Creek Trail. (see maps pages 28-29) Follow the John Muir Trail south to Shadow Lake, past the many smaller lakes–Rosalie, Gladys, and Trinity to Johnston Meadow, then Minaret Creek down to the Devils Postpile. The return to Agnew Meadows can be made via hiking or the free bus.

Lake Ediza   L. DEAN CLARK

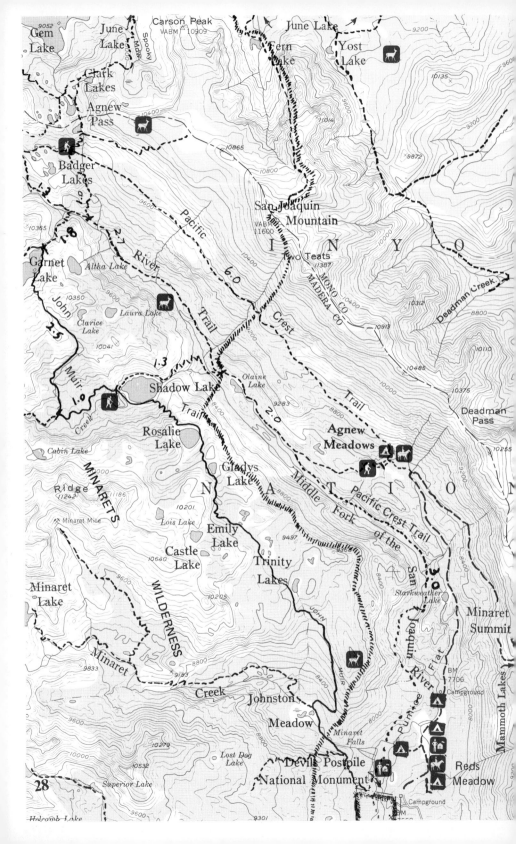

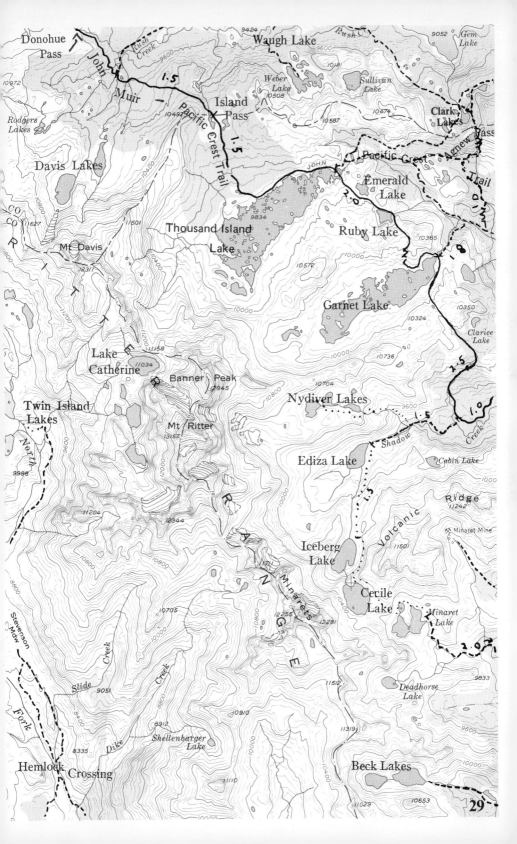

KING CREEK   3.0
"77" CORRAL   11.0
CLOVER MEADOW R.S. 22.0

MINARET WILDERNESS

L. DEAN CLARK

Westward from Devils Postpile trails lead to Snow Canyon and Summit Meadow following along the pioneer Mammoth-Postpile route to '77' Corral and Clover Meadow. The name '77' Corral was given to this high mountain meadow by the sheepmen during the drought in 1877.

Indians originally used this trail when they traded with the Monos of Owens Valley. Later when gold was discovered in Mammoth this route became the way for pack trains carrying the many supplies to the mines from the San Joaquin Valley.

From Devils Postpile to Summit Meadow the trail starts out hot and dusty. The greatest climb is beyond King Creek up to the beautiful Summit Meadow. Continuing west, it is friendly country for backpacking in contrast to the high-country, barren, exposed, windy, alpine slopes near the Minaret Crest or Iron Mountain to the north. Sheep once grazed along this trail but to save the fragile meadows and trees, there are no longer any domestic animals west of North Fork. Deer and bear are prevalent as are birds and many varieties of wildflowers. Dense stands of firs, pines, and aspens shelter the wide range of squirrels and chipmunks that make this wilderness their home.

Trails from '77' Corral lead north to Hemlock Crossing, past Iron Creek and Stevenson Meadow, up the rugged North Fork of the San Joaquin River headwaters to Twin Lakes, or turning west, to Yosemite National Park via Isberg Pass. Most of this region is above timberline.

From Summit Meadow to Beck Lakes the meadows along the trail may be boggy early in the season with many mosquitoes. Snows could make some difficulty in following the trail or cross-countrying to the upper lakes. There are no fish in Ashley or Holcomb lakes, however the impressive Iron Mountain with its glacier makes the trip worthwhile.

A good loop trip can be made via Snow Canyon, Summit Meadow, Fern Lake, with side trips to Holcomb, Ashley and Noname lakes or to Superior and Beck lakes, returning via the trail leading northeast from Beck Cabin to Minaret Falls, taking the John Muir Trail back to Devils Postpile.

FISH CREEK VALLEY

Fish Creek is one of the finest trout streams in the entire region. Along a good forest cover it meanders through the scenic mountains. This beautiful valley basin with its streams and alpine lakes of varying depth and size offers excellent fishing. As you travel south along Fish Creek the stream becomes more rapid and violent with some impassable cascades.

Originally all lakes were barren of trout. However, where the habitat is suitable, they have become established as a result of planting over a period of time. Scoop Lake is an isolated alpine lake containing Eastern Brook trout while Marsh Lakes about a mile south, have no fish. This is due to the shallow coves and grassy bays that are subject to freezing in winter killing all possible fish.

Sharktooth Creek as well as Sharktooth Lake have poor fishing. Lost Keys Lake which are in partly timbered alpine glacial benches have good self-sustaining trout and planting is only necessary occasionally.

Long Canyon Creek is a small, rapid, alpine trout stream with excellent spawning and good self-sustaining Eastern Brooks. Where Minnow Creek drops through steep cascades to Fish Creek no planting in the pools and riffles are necessary to sustain good fishing of Rainbow, Golden and Eastern Brook. In the heavier timbered areas of Minnow Creek, Long Canyon and Cascade Valley, you may find that pine martens are apt to socialize, **31** searching for food, especially trout.   L. DEAN CLARK

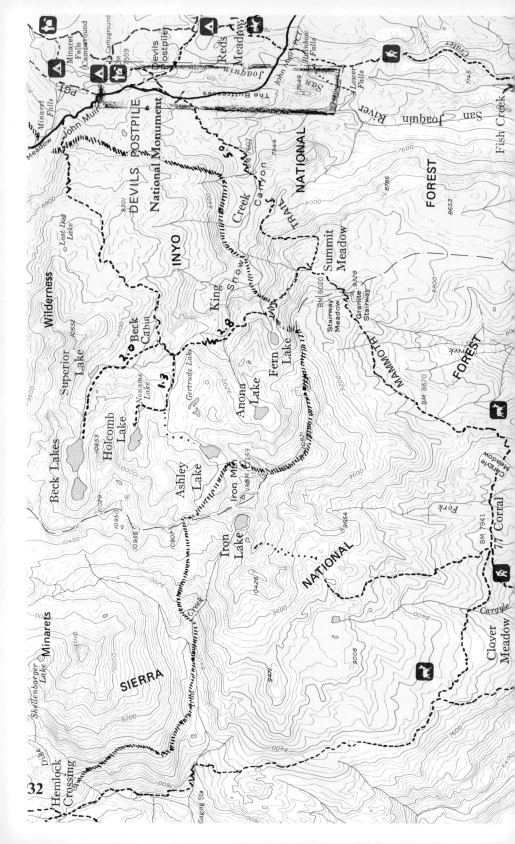

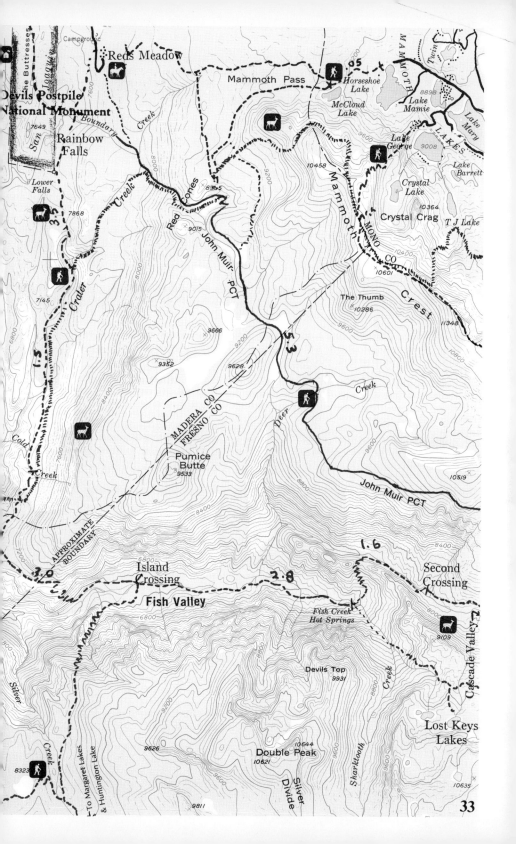

The Buttresses

Campground

Reds Meadow

Devils Postpile National Monument

Mammoth Pass

Horseshoe Lake

8898

Lake Mamie

McCloud Lake

9600

Lake Mary

Rainbow Falls

San Joaquin

Boundary

Creek

7649

Red Cones

8855

9200

10458

Lake George

9008

Crystal Lake

Lake Barrett

Lower Falls

7868

9015

John Muir·PCT

Crystal Crag

10364

T J Lake

Crater

7145

8000

8000

9566

9200

9628

5.3

The Thumb

10286

9600

Mammoth

MONO CO

10400

10601

Crest

11348

10800

Deer Creek

9382

MADERA CO FRESNO CO

Deer

Cold

Creek

7600

Pumice Butte

9533

8400

8600

John Muir PCT

10519

9600

APPROXIMATE BOUNDARY

7200

3.0

6800

Island Crossing

Fish Valley

2.8

1.6

8400

Second Crossing

8000

6800

Silver

Fish Creek Hot Springs

9109

Cascade Valley

900

9200

Devils Top

9931

Creek

Lost Keys Lakes

Creek

8323

To Margaret Lakes & Huntington Lake

9626

Double Peak

10644

10621

Silver Divide

Sharktooth

9600

10635

9811

33

MAMMOTH CREST COUNTRY

For day hikes or fishing expeditions the lakes up Coldwater Creek and to the headwaters of Mammoth Creek are extremely popular. From Lake Mary to Duck Lake it is only six miles. The trail is interesting even though it starts out dry and dusty. Part of the six miles are strenuous. It climbs over low ridges, passes through flowered mountain meadows, along the shores of Skelton, Red, and Barney lakes up to Duck Pass. These lakes below the massive Mammoth Crest are good for family fishing in a flawless natural setting. Return trips from Barney Lake are not more than five miles.

At Duck Pass is a vast panorama of the upper Owens Valley, the Basin Range country, and to the south towards the Silver Divide. The trail from Duck Pass descends and joins the John Muir-Pacific Crest Trail below Duck Lake.

The lakes between the John Muir-Pacific Crest Trail and the Mammoth Crest have excellent fishing. Deer Lakes are planted with rainbows. If you are fishing for size, the trout run smaller in Deer Creek than those in the lake.

Duck Lake (10,427'), in its moraine bed with rock and abrupt shores, has both Rainbow and Kamloop trout. Pika Lake contains Rainbow and Eastern Brooks— some as long as fourteen inches.

Purple Lake (9900') has trout averaging about a foot long. Rainbow, Eastern Brook and some Golden are taken. Up above Purple Lake close to the crest lies rockbound lakes near timberline which can be reached by cross-country trails. Glen, Horn, Hoof, Ram, Glennette and Franklin contain some Golden. Lake Virginia (10,319') was known and popularized as a Golden trout lake but now contains some Rainbow. Fingerlings are planted and grow well in this lake despite the fact it receives a great deal of traffic.

In this wilderness country there are no established campsites although most areas below and up to timberline have good places for overnight. For specifics check the Ranger when you pick up your Wilderness Permit.

34

DUCK LAKE   ROCKY ROCKWELL

MAMMOTH ROCK TRAIL

This new, easy trail starts at the Old Mammoth Road, passes under Mammoth Rock, proceeds east through the forest to the old jeep road (closed to vehicles) west of the Sherwin Creek Road. The Rock is made of limestone and marble, formed at the bottom of the ocean which once covered this entire area. Fossils in the rock have been estimated at 250 million years of age.

SHERWIN CREEK ROAD TO VALENTINE LAKE

From Mammoth Lakes, or for a day's hike from the Sherwin Creek Campground (7800') trips can be made up to Sherwin Lakes (8620'). The five lakes, 3.0 miles from the parking lot, lie close together in a basin above the moraine of the Sherwin Creek Canyon. This is a new trail. The present Sherwin Lake Trail as well as the Valentine Lake trail on the topo maps are now abandoned. This new trail goes east of Sherwin Creek with switchbacks making the climb up over the moraine less strenuous. The new trail joins the old Valentine Lake trail just past the upper Sherwin Lake. Valentine Lake (9650') carved out long ago by glaciers is truly a rock-bound pleasure. Majestic cliffs of granite confine the lake with awesome beauty. It is a good 4.5 miles from Sherwin Creek. Eastern brook trout are taken.

Valentine Lake   ROCKY ROCKWELL

Mammoth Lakes Pack Outfit operates near Lake Mary and has hourly rides around the forested basin of Mammoth Lakes and overnight trips to the John Muir Wilderness backcountry and to Valentine and Laurel lakes basin. P.O. Box 61, Mammoth Lakes, CA, 93546.

Sierra Meadows Equestrian Center features guided trail rides by the hour, or day, boarding and training facilities, riding instructions from beginners to advance equestrian. P.O. Box D-4, Mammoth Lakes, CA, 93546.

35

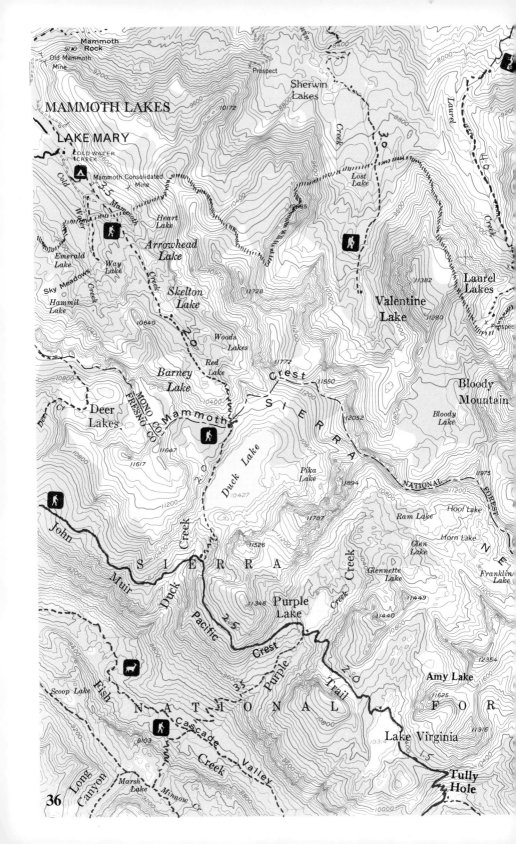

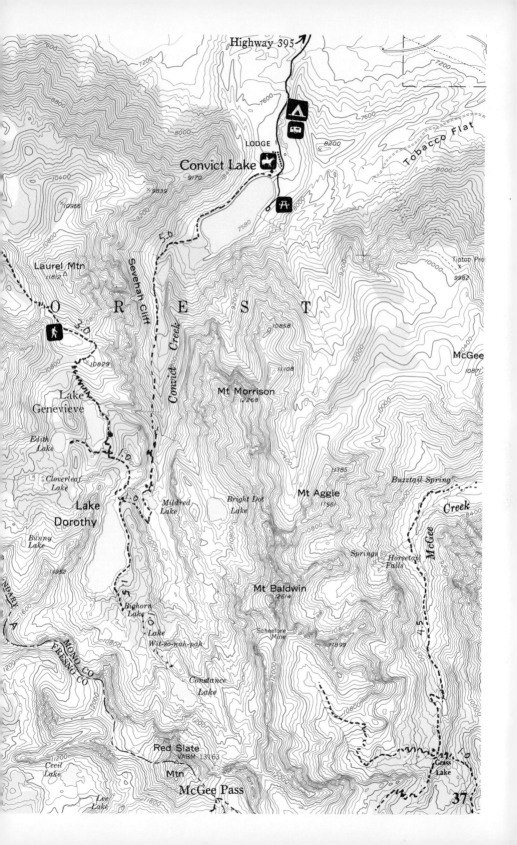

Highway 395

Tobacco Flat

LODGE

Convict Lake
9170
×9839

Laurel Mtn
11812

O R E S T

Sevehah Cliff

Convict Creek

Tiptop Pro
X
9982

McGee
10871

10400
10956
10800
10829

Lake
Genevieve

Edith
Lake

Cloverleaf
Lake

Lake
Dorothy

Bunny
Lake
11852

Mildred
Lake

Mt Morrison
12268

Bright Dot
Lake

Mt Aggie
11561

10858

11108

13385

Buzztail Spring

McGee
Creek
8400

Springs

Horsetail
Falls

Bighorn
Lake

Lake
Wit-so-nah-pak

Mt Baldwin
12614

Scheelore
Mine

11899

Constance
Lake

MONO CO
FRESNO CO

Cecil
Lake
11200

Red Slate
VABM 13163

Mtn

McGee Pass

Lee
Lake

Grass
Lake

37

CONVICT LAKE

ROCKY ROCKWELL

Some of the oldest rocks in the Sierra encircle the beautiful cool, clear blue waters of Convict Lake (7580'). This vast glacial-carved canyon with colorful rugged peaks interest the photographer as well as the fisherman. Trails lead into some great trout fishing country to the west in the higher lakes and streams below the impressive Bloody and Red Slate mountains.

Convict Lake Resort has a pack station for hour, day or more extensive rides and trips into the backcountry. Also the resort has a new cement ramp at the marina of Convict Lake, boat rentals and dockage, a restaurant, store and housekeeping cabins. Fishing for the Rainbow, Brown or Eastern Brooks at the lake is good from the shore or trolling from a private or rented boat. Motors are permitted with 10 mph max. speed. Camping is on both sides of the road leading from Hwy. 395 up the two miles into the Convict Lake area. Some of the Forest Service campsites are among the aspens by the creek while others are more exposed in a high-desert environment. There is a dumping station for RV's.

Backcountry trails from Convict Lake lead to Mildred, Genevieve and Dorothy lakes. To Lake Dorothy (10,250') it is a strenuous 6.0 mile hike but good fishing for Eastern Brooks and Rainbow. Good cross-country trails are possible to Bighorn and Constance lakes on the south of the crest, and from the north to Edith and Cloverleaf lakes.

Beyond Lake Genevieve, a steep climb leads up to the top of the ridge between Bloody and Laurel mountains. The view from this jagged alpine basin is truly fantastic. The trail continues north, down switchbacks to Laurel Canyon, then down the jeep road on the lateral moraine of Laurel Canyon to the Sherwin-Mammoth Creek road. It is a long, strenuous day for the entire loop trip, but well worth the effort. (Approx. ten miles from Convict Lake to the Laurel Canyon jeep road.)

38 Convict Lake Pack Station offers not only horseback rides around the lake but backcountry trips to Genevieve and Dorothy lakes. Convict Lake Resort, Bishop, CA, 93514.

JUNE LAKE

BACKCOUNTRY TRIPS

The Walker Lake/Bloody Canyon trail starts about a mile north of Grant Lake following the Parker Lake Trail, then northwest to Sawmill Canyon up to Walker Lake. (The trail from the roadend below Walker Lake is through private property). Beyond are the lovely Sardine Lakes below Mono Pass.

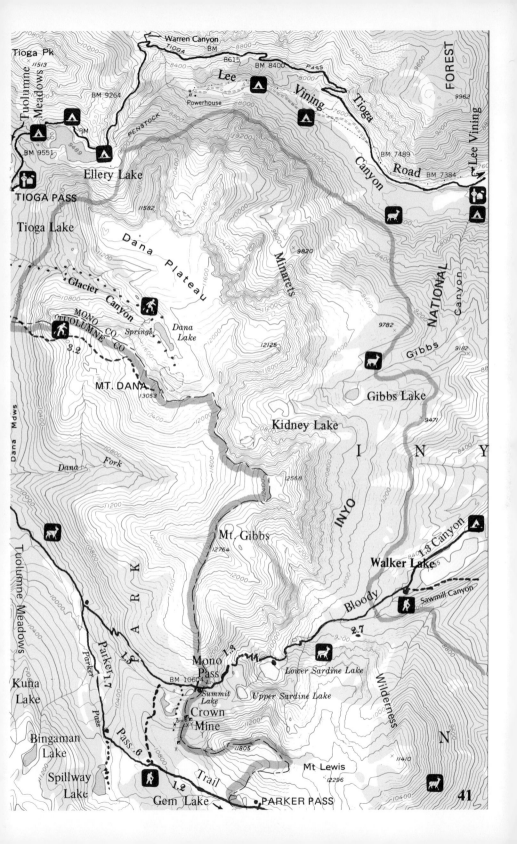

41

Bloody Canyon   ROCKY ROCKWELL

JUNE LAKE BACK COUNTRY

There are good campsites at Lower Lake Sardine and about one-fourth mile up between the Upper Sardine Lakes. There is no firewood for cooking in this glacial basin so a campstove is a necessity. The dark rocks, beautiful lakes and scrubby whitebark pines nestled close to the ground make this a true alpine adventure.

A good loop trip can be made via Walker Lane, Bloody Canyon to Mono Pass, down to Parker Pass Creek, up the Parker Pass Trail to Parker Pass, up and over Koip Pass and down to Alger and Gem Lakes, to Agnew Lake Trail back to Silver Lake.

A side excursion for fishing or backcountry photographic trip, cross-country up to Bingaman Lake or proceed further up the Parker Pass Trail to Spillway and Helen lakes. The trail over Koip Pass, around the glacial fields of Koip Peak is strenuous but extremely rewarding.

Trails lead from Mono Pass and Parker Pass west to Yosemite National Park. For further maps and guides refer to YOSEMITE TRAILS by Lew & Ginny Clark.

MINARET WILDERNESS

Beyond Agnew Lake, by crossing the Rush Creek Bridge the trail continues to climb up switchbacks to Spooky Meadows below Carson Peak. Follow the trail south to Clark Lakes. Fishing is usually rewarding. There are several good camping areas here. Check for availability of the camping sites when you secure your Wilderness Permit. See top section of map page 28 for trail. From Clark Lakes the trail leads south to Agnew Pass and into the Minarets Wilderness country.

LEE VINING CANYON

In the summer the mountain town of Lee Vining blossoms to welcome visitors and to supply vacation needs. There is camping along Lower LeeVining Creek among the aspens with no running water, primitive facilities but great fishing.

The rise from 6780' at LeeVining to 9940' at Tioga Pass may not do much for your engine on a hot summer afternoon, but the change of elevation can lift your spirits by viewing the road ahead up the canyon and looking back from the viewpoints near the top to the gray-blue distant Mono Basin beyond or straight down the canyon to the powerhouse below. Then, turning the corner you'll find beautiful Ellery Lake in its mountain splendor.

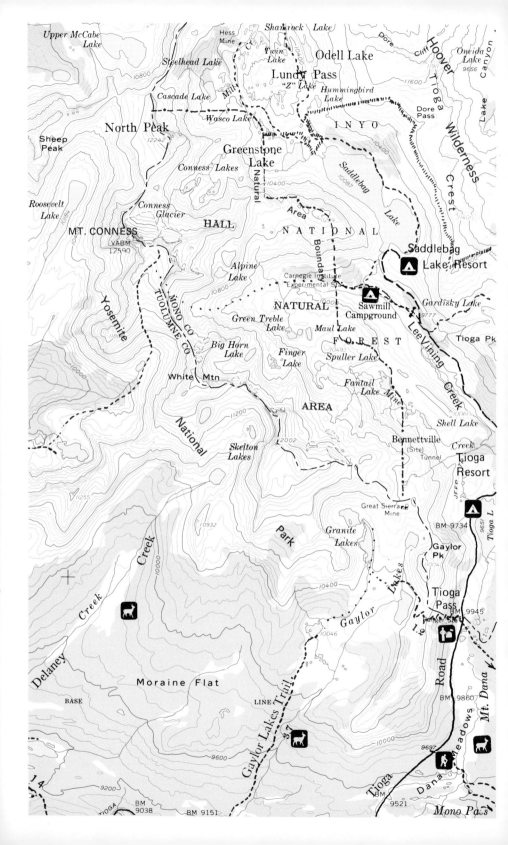

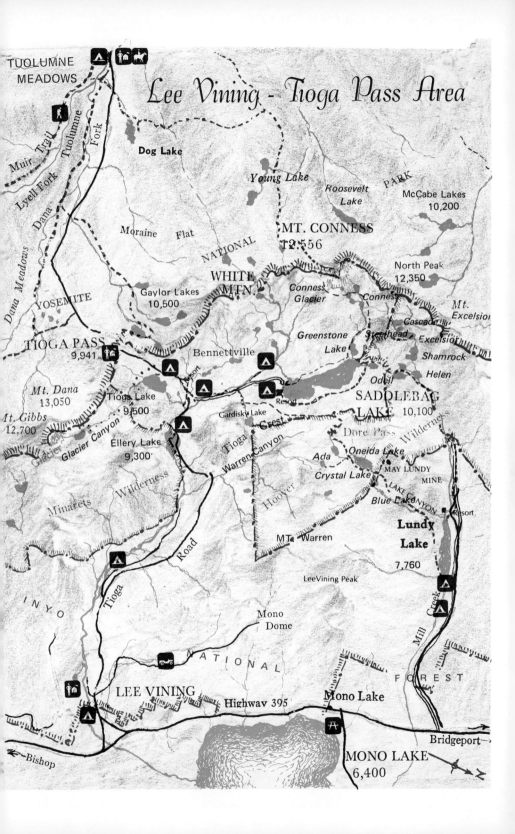

Lee Vining - Tioga Pass Area

TUOLUMNE MEADOWS

Muir Trail

Tuolumne Fork

Lyell Fork

Dana

Dana Meadows

Dog Lake

Young Lake

Roosevelt Lake

McCabe Lakes 10,200

PARK

MT. CONNESS 12,556

North Peak 12,350

Moraine Flat

NATIONAL

WHITE MTN.

Conness Glacier

Conness

Mt. Excelsior

Gaylor Lakes 10,500

Greenstone Lake

Steelhead

Cascade

Excelsior

YOSEMITE

TIOGA PASS 9,941

Bennettville

Shamrock

Helen

Mt. Dana 13,050

Resort

Odell

SADDLEBAG LAKE 10,100

Tioga Lake 9,500

Gardisky Lake

Resort

Dore Pass

Wilderness

Mt. Gibbs 12,700

Glacier Canyon

Ellery Lake 9,300

Tioga Crest

Warren Canyon

Ada

Oneida Lake

Crystal Lake

MAY LUNDY MINE

Glacier

Minarets

Wilderness

Hoover

MT. Warren

Blue Lake

LAKE CANYON

Resort

Lundy Lake 7,760

INYO

Tioga Road

LeeVining Peak

Mill Creek

Mono Dome

NATIONAL

FOREST

LEE VINING

Highway 395

Mono Lake

MONO LAKE 6,400

Bishop

Bridgeport

TIOGA - SADDLEBAG

There are public campgrounds along Ellery Lake and near Tioga Pass Resort at the junction to Saddlebag Lake. Forest Service campsites are for RV's or tents and walk-in camps are along the upper LeeVining Creek. Fishing is good at Ellery, Tioga, and Saddlebag lakes, LeeVining Creek, and at the numerous lakes in the Hall Natural Area below the imposing White Mountain and Mt. Conness.

The magnificent Mt. Conness and surrounding peaks of the Yosemite National Park boundary capture the interest of the photographer as moods change from hour to hour, day to day with shadows and sunlight.

Tioga Pass Resort rents housekeeping cabins, boats and motors (for the several lakes nearby), serves home-style meals, supplies the visitor with film, gifts, fishing tackle, reading material in their store, sells gasoline, and gives helpful suggestions.

Saddlebag Resort has a good marina, store and restaurant. Boat trips can be made to the other end of the lake. The campground is open, among junipers, windy, with a high-mountain, vigorous atmosphere that is so different from sleeping along the creek among peaceful aspens.

From Tioga Pass Resort or Saddlebag Lake there are day hikes for fishing or appreciating the mountain environment:

Visit the Tioga mine and ghost town of Bennettville.

Walk the Tioga Tarns Nature Trail.

Hike up Warren Canyon, one of the most beautiful in the Sierra. A good loop trip could be made by going west up to Gardisky Lake, then down to Saddlebag Lake.

Climb up to the Gaylor-Granite Lakes from Tioga Pass. Parking area near the checking station. It is a steep ascend but the views from these lakes are fabulous. The fishing is good, too.

Hike up Glacier Canyon from lower Tioga Lake, passing several little lakes to Dana Lake, then beyond to the Dana Glacier. Mountain climbers practice scaling on the rugged northeast face of Mt. Dana from here.

The lakes between the LeeVining Canyon and White Mountain on the Yosemite National Park boundary are easy to cross country and are most beautiful in their alpine setting.

46 There is a good but steep cross-country trail to the Conness Glacier.

MT. CONNESS - GREENSTONE LAKE   ROCKY ROCKWELL

ONEIDA LAKE   ROCKY ROCKWELL

LUNDY CANYON

At the north end of our MAMMOTH-MONO COUNTRY is Lundy Canyon. This is an ideal mountain vacation spot, particularly if you enjoy a more rustic, quiet atmosphere. There is good camping under the aspens along Mill Creek below Lundy Lake where each year fishermen stay for a period of time in their old haunts.

The Lundy Lake Resort offers camping at the head of the lake with spaces looking down the canyon into the valley below eastward towards Bodie. There are tables, showers, and laundry facilities as well as housekeeping cabins, restaurant, store, gasoline, and a trailer park for those wishing hookups. They generate their own power to serve the resort.

This canyon is especially beautiful in the autumn when the aspen leaves turn into gorgeous orange and yellow to contrast the green pines and colored rocks on the surrounding slopes. Wildflowers adorn the fields all summer and cool breezes make the nights refreshing.

Fishing in the lake is exceptional from the shore as well as from a boat. It is well stocked throughout the summer into the fall. There is also good fishing in the streams and up in the beaver ponds. These beavers were first introduced into this canyon in the 1940's.

A trip up-canyon is well worth any scratches you may receive on your car — at times the road narrows to a one-lane affair. Trails from here lead past three falls to Helen, Shamrock, Steelhead, Twin and Odell lakes, and to Lundy Pass (3.5 miles). Other lakes in the upper headwater basin at the base of North Peak are Cascade, "Z", Wasco, Hummingbird. Below beautiful Mt. Conness are the Conness Lakes, Greenstone, and Saddlebag Lakes (4.5 miles).

From the south side of Lundy Lake, trails lead up the open talus slopes to Lake Canyon along the South Fork of Mill Creek. Blue, Crystal, Oneida and Ada lakes provide beauty and fishing. To the west of this chain of mountain lakes is the old May Lundy Mine.

Auto tours include trips to Bodie, Virginia Lakes, the town of Bridgeport, Twin Lakes, Dogtown, Mono Lake, up Tioga Pass Road to Tuolumne **47** Meadows in Yosemite National Park or one of the day hikes around or to lakes near Tioga Pass.

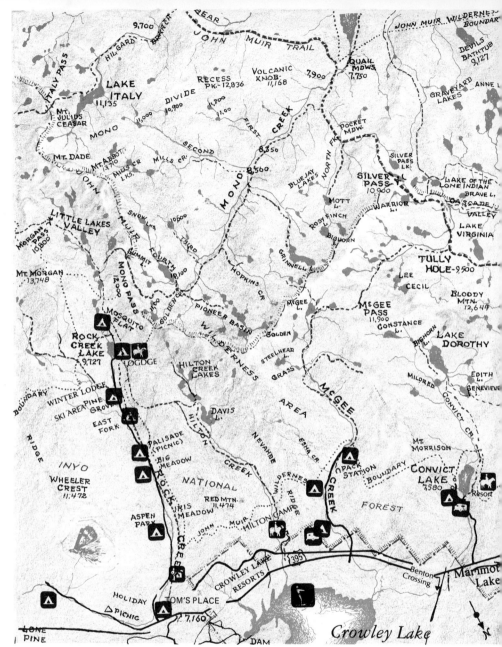

ROCK CREEK COUNTRY

The Rock Creek roadhead at 10,400' is one of the highest in the Sierra. Because of the easy approach to the Mono Creek Basin from the John Muir Trail it is a heavily used area. Firewood is scarce so chemical fuel campstoves are necessary. Be sure to check with the Ranger when you secure your Wilderness Permit for available overnight camp sites. Because of the many lakes and basins, there are places that are not too crowded. For instance in the second Recess area, to get off the beaten track cross-country is possible by following the contour of the land, old abandoned trails and ducked routes.

ROCK CREEK CANYON

Climbing westward from Tom's Place up through the sagebrush and pinyon pines, the blue haze of the Owens Valley is soon far below.

Beyond the Rock Creek Canyon Entrance Station are many campsites beneath lodgepoles and fluttering aspens along the creek. The roadend of Rock Creek (10,250') is higher than Tioga Pass or Whitney Portal and is the highest of the eastern entries to the Sierra backcountry.

The variety of lakes in size and environment; the extensiveness of the territory beyond the several mountain passes to routes of trans-Sierra or north and south via John Muir and Pacific Crest Trail; or trails leading to alpine basins high up in the granite-walled canyons above timberline make this approach unsurpassed.

About ten miles from Hwy. 395, high in the clear, sparkling crisp air are two resorts. The Rock Creek Lodge, left of the road through the Pine Grove Campground, past the creek, offers gasoline, ice, groceries, fishing supplies, restaurant, cabins, showers but no telephone. The Rock Creek Lake Resort, a little further up the road on the right side provides gasoline, ice, groceries, fishing supplies, cabins, showers, propane, and boat rentals. No telephone.

Rock Creek Pack Station offers High Sierra Trail Rides into the Little Lakes Valley, over Morgan Pass, over Mono Pass into the incredible fishing country of the basins to the west of the Sierra Crest. They also feature the annual Owens Valley Horse Drive and Trail Ride. Box 248, Bishop, CA, 93514.

Trails lead into the vast John Muir Wilderness backcountry from Pine Grove campground to Tamarack Lakes, or from the Mosquito trailhead (parking) into the magnificent Little Lakes Valley, over Morgan Pass to Pine Creek, or over Mono Pass to the Recesses, Pioneer Basin and Hopkins **49** Creek. Trails lead north over a ridge to gain elevation for the Hilton Creek lakes.

McGEE CREEK CANYON

The unimposing entrance to the McGee Creek country is deceiving. The further into the canyon below Mt. Crocker and the Red and White Mountain the more spectacular the area with the coloration of the gray and red ridge of Mt. Baldwin with the Red Slate and the Red and White mountains. McGee Pass is in the saddle between these two mountains. The long, hot dusty way up through the pinyon-sagebrush high-desert should begin early in the morning. Fishing is excellent at Little McGee, Crocker, and Golden lakes. Over McGee Pass the trail leads to Upper Fish Creek with fabulous fishing. Many trips are available to the north, west and south. The junction to the John Muir Trail is about 5.0 miles from McGee Pass. The best approach to climb Red Slate, Red and White Mountain, or Stanford Peak is from this area.

The 1980 earthquake did not change the trails. There are several Forest Service campgrounds on the road up to the pack station. They are situated among the aspens along McGee Creek.

HILTON CREEK

Lovely Hilton Creek bordered with beautiful aspens is especially grand in the autumn. The trail from here leads to the upper basin headwaters past Davis Lake to the cluster of ten Hilton Creek Lakes below Mt. Huntington and Stanford Peak.

To avoid the high desert-sagebrush portion of the lower Hilton Creek Trail to the upper lakes, the trail from Rock Creek starts higher with a small climb over the divide that separates the two basins.

McGEE CREEK CANYON   ROCKY ROCKWELL

McGee Pack Station is at the end of the dirt road approximately 4.0 miles from Hwy. 395. They pack up into McGee Canyon, over McGee Pass into the Upper Fish Creek area, with spot trips, the All Expense Trip, the Extended Trip, and the Dunnage Pack. McGee Pack Station, Box 1054, Bishop, CA, 93514.

Kyte's Hilton Lakes Camp and Pack Station is a half mile west of Hwy. 395. Their trips cover the Hilton Lakes basin. The Base Camp is at 7200', offers housekeeping cabins, dormitory accommodations, evening campfire programs as well as riding and fishing. Rte. 3, Box 156, Bishop, CA, 93514.

CROWLEY LAKE

One of the finest lakes for fishing in California! Thousands come here on every opening day of the fishing season. Crowley Lake is administrated by the City of Los Angeles, Dept. of Recreation and Parks. They operate all the boating and fishing facilities at the lake and provide life-guard protection for the public. Because this is a reservoir for the domestic water supply of Los Angeles, certain restrictions are necessary.

Water skiing is permitted on the lake. Boats can be rented and reserved. Permit fees for private boats include inspection and launching. There is private boat storage available and vehicle parking. (No charge, however, to park if your private boat or city rental boat fee has been paid.) Because gusts of winds from the desert and mountains are sudden and sometimes extremely strong, for safety, no boat less than twelve feet is allowed to be launched nor rubber rafts, canoes, or canvas boats.

Crowley Lake Store issues fishing licenses, supplies, bait, lures, information, and up-to-date regulations. Camp High Sierra offers wooded areas for campers with trailers, RV's or tents and have cabins, a recreational lodge, hot showers, and dumping facilities. Crowley Lake Resort has trailer rentals and housekeeping units.

There are four basic methods of fishing in Crowley Lake: trolling with lures; baitfishing on or off shore with cheese-bait or a combination cheese-egg-bait; lure fishing from the shore; fly fishing on or off the shore. The regular special fly fishing season is in late summer and is an excellent sport. For more specific information on the most successful bait and lures to use, visit Crowley Lake Store or one of the good sport stores in Mammoth Lakes or Bishop.

For diversified fishing, try the Owens River at Benton Crossing. This popular stream supports Rainbow and Brown trout. From Owens River out in the desert of Long Valley, imposing views are of the Sierra to the west and of the White Mountains to the east.

To reach Benton Crossing, turn east about one mile south of the Convict Lake turnoff of Hwy. 395. About one mile in from the Highway is WHITMORE HOT SPRINGS which offers a cool refreshing stop with a swim 51 in the pool. The road going east services the North and East Landings of Crowley Lake and further on to Watterson Canyon.

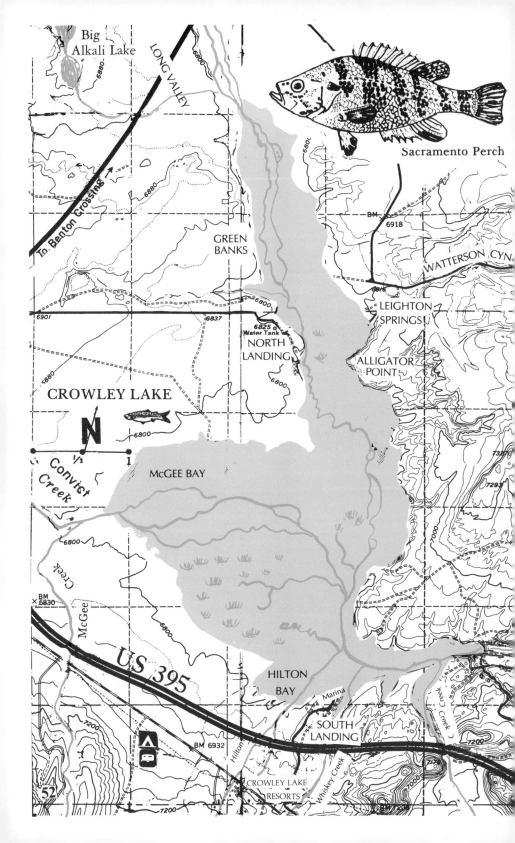

Big
Alkali Lake

LONG VALLEY

Tn. Benton Crossing

6901

6880

6880

6800

GREEN
BANKS

6837

6825
Water Tank
NORTH
LANDING

6800

6800

Sacramento Perch

BM
6918

WATTERSON CYN.

LEIGHTON
SPRINGS

ALLIGATOR
POINT

7380

CROWLEY LAKE

N

1/2   1

Convict
Creek

6800

McGEE BAY

7293

Creek

BM
6830

McGee

6800

US 395

7200

HILTON
BAY

Marina

Whiskey Creek

SOUTH
LANDING

BM 6932

Hilton

7200

7000

CROWLEY LAKE
RESORTS

7200

52

FISHERMEN'S NOTES

The three most popular fish taken from Crowley Lake are the Rainbow and Brown Trout and the Sacramento Perch

RAINBOW TROUT average weight is one pound, about eleven inches long. Two sub-species are also found in the lake: Kamloops, a very active sportfish with vivid colored coppery gills; Eagle Lake Trout similar to the Cutthroat in appearance, and a little shy about being caught!

BROWN TROUT comes BIG. Each year trophy size browns range from eight to nine pounds. They are easily distinguishable with red and dark brown spots on the lighter brown skin.

SACRAMENTO PERCH are usually ten to eleven inches long to about one to two pounds. There is no limit to the number of perch you can catch. They are delicious eating whether fried, smoked or barbecued.

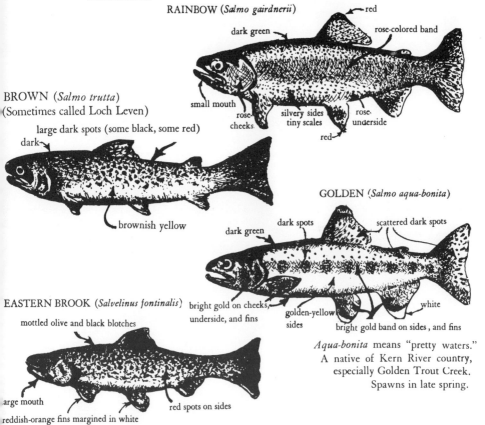

RAINBOW (*Salmo gairdnerii*)

red

dark green

rose-colored band

BROWN (*Salmo trutta*)
(Sometimes called Loch Leven)

large dark spots (some black, some red)

dark

small mouth

rose-cheeks

silvery sides
tiny scales

rose-underside

red

brownish yellow

GOLDEN (*Salmo aqua-bonita*)

dark green

dark spots

scattered dark spots

EASTERN BROOK (*Salvelinus fontinalis*)

mottled olive and black blotches

bright gold on cheeks, underside, and fins

golden-yellow sides

white

bright gold band on sides, and fins

Aqua-bonita means "pretty waters." A native of Kern River country, especially Golden Trout Creek. Spawns in late spring.

large mouth

red spots on sides

reddish-orange fins margined in white

A heavy-bodied, large-mouthed trout. Common above 7,000 ft. Usually frequents deeper holes and slower-moving water than Rainbow. Spawns in the fall.

Fishermen, sometimes, have a bad reputation for littering cans, bottles, bait containers and other trash. It only takes a few scattered papers and containers to make a mess. Valuable game fish die because they swallow pop tabs from cans. Children as well as adults cut feet from wading in streams or along the lakeshore 53 from broken glass. Please help save ourselves, the fish we like to catch, our beautiful forests, lakes, and streams by packing out all the litter you pack in.

AROUND MAMMOTH LAKES

The fishing. The views. The beauty of the lakes. The history and the ghost towns. The geologic wonders ... all make Mammoth Lakes a wonderful vacation land. There are many interesting things to see and do.

From the summit of the San Joaquin Ridge is a magnificent panorama of the Ritter Range with the canyon headwaters of the Middle Fork of the San Joaquin River below. The MINARET VISTA is about a mile west of the Mammoth Mountain Ski Area. The Forest Service has provided picnic tables and a self-guiding tour identifying trees and shrubs in the area as well as geologic rocks and the outstanding vista points. There is a 2.5 mile trail along the Ridge for those wishing to explore more and have a good, short walk.

The EARTHQUAKE FAULT, on the Minaret Road west of Mammoth Lakes, has an exhibit describing this particular geological break of 55 ft. in the earth's surface. A short nature trail leads down through the crack.

PANORAMA DOME   A walk through the forest of a 1.5 mi. loop trip leads to a fine panorama view of the Mammoth Lakes Basin.

CRYSTAL CRAG   dominates the Basin. It was formed by the glacial quarrying of the ridge which once separated the drainages of Crystal and T.J. Lakes.

The Mammoth Mountain Ski Area is open during the summer to provide gondola rides to the top of Mammoth Mountain. Also open is the cafeteria and sport shop. From the top of the mountain the expansive basin of the entire MAMMOTH - MONO COUNTRY lies below ... Long Valley and Crowley Lake; San Joaquin Range, over to June Mountain north to Mono Lake; the Ritter Range and the forested San Joaquin River basin. A walk out to the south from the ski life boarding area offers a view of the Mammoth Lakes Basin, Crystal Crag, and the Mammoth Crest. Mammoth Mountain is an inactive volcanic peak, ideal for excellent winter and spring skiing.

Picnics are always enjoyable. With the variety of places in this region for picnics, you could enjoy one in a different atmosphere and surroundings every day: at the Minaret Vista with its spectacular view, under the jeffrey pines along the shores of a Mammoth Lake or by Twin Falls; at a ghost town site of old mining days; at Devils Postpile, Sotcher Lake, or Rainbow Falls; or in the Deadman Recreation Area. For a complete list, check at the Visitor 55 Center.

BATHHOUSE AT REDS MEADOW HOT SPRINGS   L. DEAN CLARK

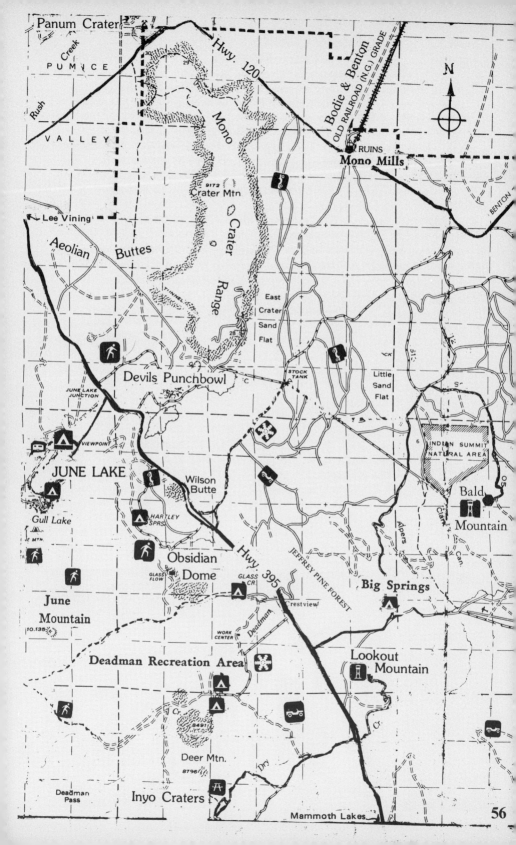

Panum Crater

Creek

PUMICE

Rush

VALLEY

Lee Vining

Aeolian Buttes

Crater Mtn 9172

Mono Crater Range

Hwy. 120

Bodie & Benton
OLD RAILROAD (N.G.) GRADE

N

RUINS
Mono Mills

BENTON

East
Crater
Sand
Flat

TUNNEL

STOCK
TANK

Little
Sand
Flat

Devils Punchbowl

JUNE LAKE JUNCTION

VIEWPOINT

INDIAN SUMMIT
NATURAL AREA

JUNE LAKE

Wilson
Butte

Bald
Mountain

Gull Lake

HARTLEY
SPRS.

GLASS
FLOW

Obsidian
Dome

GLASS
CR.

Hwy. 395

Crestview

JEFFREY PINE FOREST

Alpers Can.

Clark Can.

Big Springs

June
Mountain

10,135

Deadman

WORK
CENTER

Deadman Recreation Area

Lookout
Mountain

Cr.

8491

Deer Mtn.
8796

Dry

Deadman
Pass

Inyo Craters

Mammoth Lakes

56

There are many jeep roads as indicated on the maps pages 56 and 64 . On all these pumicite and soft-soil roads a four-wheel drive, or at least a pickup is recommended. Smaller, lighter weight cars are apt to get stuck in the dusty pumice. Even though the roads may be packed well, stay on the road! If it rains or if the road is wet, it could be slippery.

OBSIDIAN DOME turnoff is about 15 miles north of Mammoth Lakes and is well marked. There are foot trails all through the sharp rocks. A careful scramble up the rocks leads to photographic and view points of the country to the east and south. Around to the west and south of the Dome are roads leading to pleasant places for picnics under the pines.

Pure obsidian is black, although it is also found in a black and brown mixture. Obsidian is the result of rapidly cooling lava which turned to glass. White streaks or flakes found in the black glass was froth in the hot liquid stage. The rock-shaped pumice that looks like petrified sponge is a volcanic glass, full of cavities, and very light in weight. Light enough to float in water. Pumicite is a fine powdery pumice dust, which is spread all over this country.

DEVILS PUNCHBOWL is a small but well-preserved explosion cone. Its crater is 1200' in diameter and 140' deep. In the bottom is a small obsidian plug 40' high and 250' in diameter.

INYO CRATERS have the distinction of being the youngest crater of this Mono group. Debris from these craters covered the land for miles around exemplifying the tremendous force of this volcanic action. Unlike most craters, they hold water. Don't plan on catching fish here as there are none. The road leading to the craters is well marked. There is good parking and a picnic area. A self-guiding trail makes the tour informative and interesting. 57

OBSIDIAN DOME   ROCKY ROCKWELL

HOT CREEK is the best hot springs to visit. A large parking area is provided to view this geothermal site. NOTE: Swimming is not recommended due to natural hazards — the ground is extremely unstable and the water extremely hot.

Visit the FISH HATCHERY on the way to the hot springs. Besides breeding stock, the catchable trout are raised here to be planted into the many lakes and streams for your bait. The springs provide the necessary temperature for nurturing these fingerlings so they can grow all year round.

There are several other fish hatcheries on the east side of the Sierra. The streams and lakes are relatively unproductive and some do not have the capability to produce and support large populations of trout. The California Fish and Game stock lakes and streams with fingerlings as well as thousands of catchable size trout throughout the fishing season. Backcountry lakes are stocked with fingerlings every two or three years as most of these high country lakes provide sufficient spawning beds for the trout.

LOOKOUT MOUNTAIN (8352') presents a good vantage point to view the surrounding country from the Sierra peaks to the west, south to Crowley Lake and as far east as the White Mountains. The road is dirt, and steep, rising up 1000 feet through the Jeffrey Pine Forest.

WILSON BUTTE can be seen from the highway to the west. It is similar to the Mono Craters in its formation. A jeep road follows behind the Butte to the campground at HARTLEY SPRINGS. This road is a cross-country ski trail in the winter.

Another lookout point is from BALD MOUNTAIN (9104') which is north of Lookout Mountain and east of the Wilson Butte, near the Indiana Summit Natural Area. The turnoff is marked on the highway. The dirt road under normal conditions can be made by cars. It is about two miles in from the highway through logging so watch out for trucks. The last half mile becomes sharp with obsidian chips covering the roadbed.

58

MAMMOTH VISTA   TOM JOHNSTON, MAMMOTH MOUNTAIN

JEFFREY PINE FOREST

Between Mammoth Lake and June Lake is the largest Jeffrey Pine Forest in the world. It is one of the more stately members of the pine family. They grow tall in the pumice soil–from 75' to 175' and 1½' to 4' in diameter. They were in great demand by the early sawmills for their straight, large bodied characteristics. Some grow to be over four hundred years old. Needles are in bunches of three, blue-green in color, usually between 7" to 11" long. The bark is reddish-brown, thick with rough, narrow furrows in young trees, smoother in older. There is a strong vanilla or pineapple odor about them. Their cones are large 3" to 6" in diameter, 5" to 11" long with a purplish cast. The end prickles turn inward and do not hurt when handled.

The Piuga worms infestate the Jeffrey pine but they do not kill the tree. The Pandora moth developed from these worms was food for early man. Indians lived among these pines as wickiups and other camping evidences were found.

59

ROCKY ROCKWELL

MONO CRATERS

Mono Craters were formed when the volcanic fires cooled after the Ice Age. These three gray cones east of the Sierra Nevada extend southward for some ten miles. Domes of volcanic glass (obsidian) have risen in their center from the bowels of each crater. Pumice and ash were blown out and strewn for miles around. Pumice fragments and dust cover the landscape as far away as thirty miles and as deep as twenty feet east of the craters.

Mono Lake, just north of the craters, lies in a fault basin surrounded by their volcanic debris. Old wave markings indicate a shoreline when it was considerably larger and almost one thousand feet deep. The fresh waters of the ancient lake came from the melting glaciers between Rush Creek and the Conway Summit. Today the waters are saltier than the ocean. Countless brine shrimp and flies are food for millions of shorebirds including gulls, grebes, avocets, and phalaropes.

L. DEAN CLARK

MONO LAKES

There are two islands in the lake, which were formed by volcanic eruptions in the old lakebed area that was an extension of the activity at Mono Craters. Paoha, the largest island has cold and hot flowing springs and a small lake in its volcanic formed crater. The smaller island, Negit, is the home of the largest sea gull rookery in the west.

The tufa towers of Mono Lake were made up of the accumulation of plant life around upflowing calcareous waters from fresh water springs out of the bottom of the lake. When exposed to the air, they became solidified into their present interesting sculpture-like forms.

The controversy of Mono Lake has become more vocal as the lake deteriorates. Waters that normally would empty into this lake basin have been diverted and a sterile, white alkaline-encrusted lake-bottom is left along its receding shores.

Quoting from the Mono Lake Committee flyer: *"Unless diversions are curtailed, Mono Lake will shrink into a sterile chemical sump too salty and alkaline for birds or the invertebrates on which they feed. Alkali dust blowing off 30,000 acres of exposed lake bottom will endanger people, plants, and wildlife far from the lake itself. The result will be a major ecological disaster. Only by maintaining Mono at or above 6378 feet can we assure our descendants, not a wasteland, but a living lake set in the midst of natural splendor."*

60

DOGTOWN   L. DEAN CLARK

GOLD MINES AND GHOST TOWNS

Gold does not exist indiscriminately in native rock. It was deposited in definite zones by relief of pressure from within the earth through openings or weaknesses of the rock. Faulting and earth movements during the violent beginning of the formation of the Sierra created many weaknesses. Pure gold is rare as it is found combined with pyrite, iron oxides and many other minerals. Lodes are found in streaks or veins and claims were placed where prospectors felt veins should be. In the May Lundy Mine, gold was found in hornblende granite which consisted of some free gold and some pyrite. At Bennettville, claims were located near surface quartz veins and the mineralized metamorphic rocks. In the Mammoth Mining District gold was found in bunches and spots of iron oxide, and other minerals mixed with the native gold.

Ghost towns and gold mines had interesting names: Blind Springs Hills, Blue Bird Lode, Clover Patch, Contention, Don Quixote, East Noonday, Gazelle, Jump Up Joe, Lady Locke, Lizzie, Lost Horse, Rattlesnake, Sour Dough, and Twenty Grand. The most commanding was near Bennettville, now a ghost town a mile west of Tioga Lodge. The Great Sierra Consolidated Mining Company was formed. The road that was built to service the mill, The Great Sierra Wagon Road, is now Hwy. 120 over Tioga Pass to Yosemite. They built the Great Sierra Tunnel, driven some 1785' into the mountain to locate the main lode. They even had a Great Sierra Telephone Line between Lundy and Bennettville. Actually, they were long on names but short on value received.

Other mine sites and ghost towns to visit are Dogtown, Masonic, Aurora, China Camp Diggings, Mono Diggings, and of course, Bodie. In Nevada, east and northeast of Bridgeport up in the Sweetwater Mountains, there were many claims with many smaller placer mines in the Sweetwater Creek.

Aurora was well-known and became a town of some two thousand citizens. At one time it was the Mono County Seat. Nevada declared Aurora the Esmeralda County Seat, but after a long two years, the survey officials set the boundary line of the states four miles west of Aurora. By wagon the records and equipment of the Mono County government was moved to Bodie, then later to Bridgeport, the present Mono County seat.

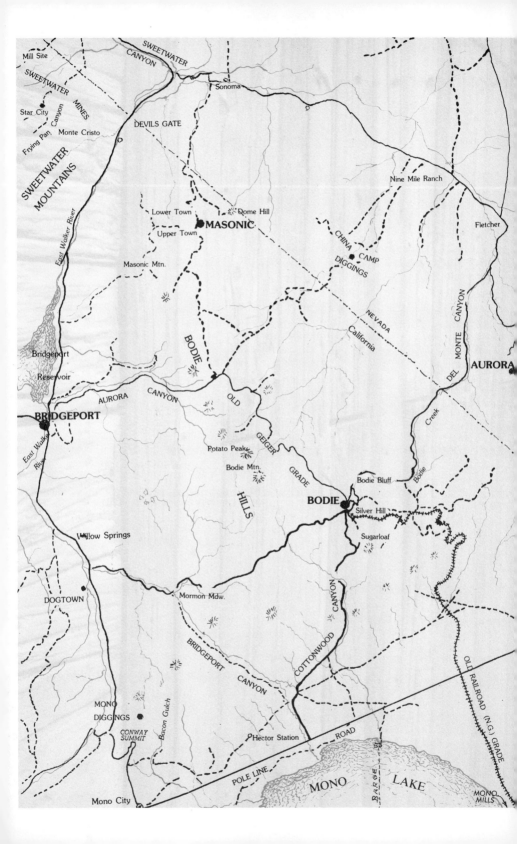

BODIE

In July, 1859 William Bodie and a few companions were exploring the hills north of Mono Lake. Prospectors were searching everywhere east of the Sierra as traces were found at Dogtown and Monoville. Bodie and his companions found evidences of placer gold and built a cabin. The winter proved too severe and they headed out for Monoville. Bodie became ill and died. It was not until the summer of 1871 that the winter grave was found and Bodie's remains were brought back to the site where he had found his gold.

In the spring following his death, claims were stacked and a district organized. Activity was minor until 1872 when rich ore was found in shallow deposits. Of the seven hundred locations, less than half a dozen were sound with only the Bodie, the Standard Mine, and the Bulwar profitable.

By 1879 the town grew to about five thousand. Fifteen to twenty freight teams were required to haul in the necessary supplies. There were several daily stages that ran to Aurora and Bridgeport. With some two dozen saloons, and almost as many lawyers, the long, cold winters with idle men led to lawlessness that merited the expression, "The Bad Men of Bodie." Stage robberies and killings were a daily occurrence.

A narrow-gauge railroad was built between Bodie and Mono Mills, south of Mono Lake to haul in the much needed wood from the Jeffrey Pine forest. It took unbelievable quantities of wood to keep the mines operating and the people warm.

Peak production was in 1881 when ten to twelve thousand people lived in Bodie. In 1893 it became one of the first mining camps to use electricity. After 1912 there was reduced activity as many mines folded and the railroad was abandoned. A severe fire destroyed most of the town in 1932. The Bureau of Mines reports that Bodie produced more than $30 million in gold and yielded over one **65** million ounces of silver.

ERNEST HOMMERDING

WINTER IN MAMMOTH

The massive Mammoth Mountain is well named. With such great snowfall annually the season is one of the longest in the country, starting in the middle of November until May or June. Mammoth Mountain (11,053') has many kinds of runs with vertical drops of varying degree. The bottom runs are more gentle and gradual for beginners and intermediates. At the top the runs are steep for the experts only. The depth of snow is never a problem — but the amount, too much, sometimes is. With such a wide and open area on this mountain, there is room for all. Ski patrols, avalanche control, first aid centers and traffic and line control are there to help you.

If you are not accustomed to the snow and sun combination, beware! Good sun glasses are necessary to protect your eyes. A lotion for dry, sensitive skin is a must to soften the harshness of wind, sun and snow glare on your face. Lips become very dry and need a moistener.

Cars need attention also. Chains, ice scrapper, and a good battery are important. Remember the mountain air with the extreme cold affects your carburetor and needs more air to offset the rarified oxygen.

MAMMOTH SKI SCHOOL has many types of classes: 3-day beginner package, private lessons, weekend specials, Funland for the pre-schooler's, Children's Ski School for ages 6-12, advanced ski clinic, and racing. P.O. Box 24, Mammoth Lakes, CA, 93546.

On Mammoth Mountain there are sixteen chair, two gondola, two T-Bar lifts and a Poma lift for the very young set right behind the mid-station.

There are two ski touring centers with complete Nordic expert instruction, guided tours, equipment rental, winter survival classes and warming huts.

MAMMOTH SKI TOURING CENTER is at the Village Center Mall and at Tamarack Lodge (at Twin Lakes) using the Lake Mary Warming Hut. Tamarack Lodge, P.O. Box 69, Mammoth Lakes, CA, 94546.

SIERRA MEADOWS SKI TOURING is located on the Old Mammoth Road past The Stove and left at the Y. They host the FWSIA Exams and Clinic in the early spring. Hot lunches and drinks are available in their own warming hut. Box D-4, Mammoth Lakes, CA, 93546.

The Forest Service supervises four main ski trails behind the Visitor Center in the Shady Rest Campground area. The trees and road of the campground make this an ideal shelter to ski in stormy weather. Snowmobile routes follow the existing roads throughout the entire region.

Ski tours via helicopters are new. They can whirl you to the top of San Joaquin Mountain or other nearby peaks. Helicopters are used for avalanche alert and control. Be sure to check with the Forest Ranger for possible **67** avalanche activity when you sign out to ski, especially any cross-country trails.

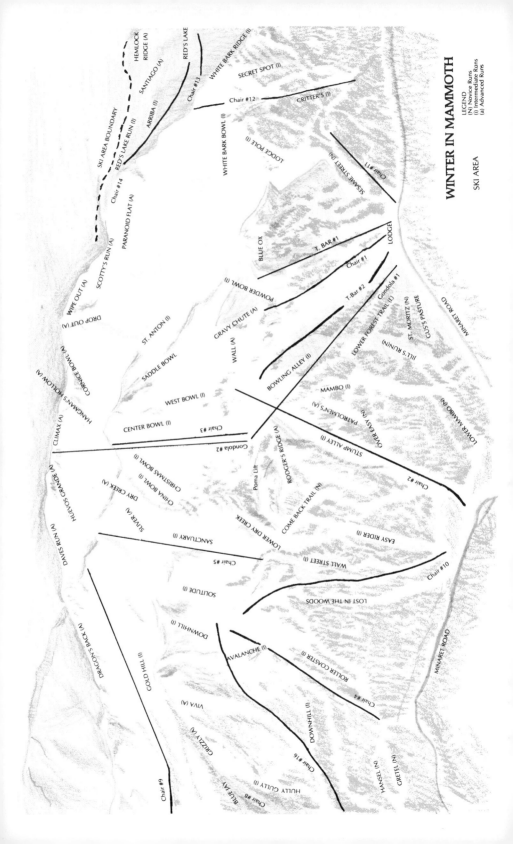

WINTER IN MAMMOTH

SKI AREA

LEGEND
(N) Novice Runs
(i) Intermediate Runs
(a) Advanced Runs

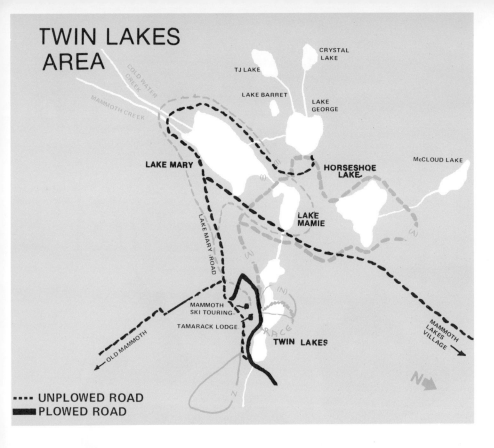

TWIN LAKES AREA

CRYSTAL LAKE

TJ LAKE

LAKE BARRET

LAKE GEORGE

McCLOUD LAKE

COLD WATER CREEK

MAMMOTH CREEK

LAKE MARY

HORSESHOE LAKE

(I)

LAKE MARY ROAD

LAKE MAMIE

(A)

(N)

MAMMOTH SKI TOURING

TAMARACK LODGE

RACE

TWIN LAKES

OLD MAMMOTH

MAMMOTH LAKES VILLAGE →

N

- - - - **UNPLOWED ROAD**
▬▬▬▬ **PLOWED ROAD**

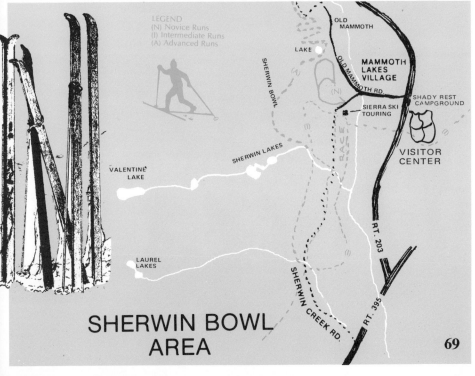

LEGEND
(N) Novice Runs
(I) Intermediate Runs
(A) Advanced Runs

OLD MAMMOTH

LAKE

SHERWIN BOWL

OLD MAMMOTH RD.

MAMMOTH LAKES VILLAGE

SHADY REST CAMPGROUND

(A)

(N)

SIERRA SKI TOURING

RACE

SHERWIN LAKES

VISITOR CENTER

VALENTINE LAKE

(I)

(I)

RT. 203

LAUREL LAKES

(I)

SHERWIN CREEK RD.

RT. 395

SHERWIN BOWL AREA

69

All photographs by   TOM JOHNSTON, MAMMOTH MOUNTAIN

RAINBOW SUMMIT

SKI AREA BOUNDARY

SCHATZI - EAST (A)

SCHATZI - WEST (A)

DEER CHUTE

DAVOS DROP

POWDER CHUTE

ROSA MAE (L)

LOTTIE JOHL (I)

BODIE (I)

SUN RISE (I)

SUNSET (A)

SILVERADO (N)

SCHATZI (I)

Chair #3

MATTERHORN (A)

SKI AREA BOUNDARY

Hutson Haus

BUNKER HILL

Chair #4 & Reload Station

RIVER RUN (N)

MAMBO (N)

CHALET (I)

SURPISE (I)

SKI AREA BOUNDARY

NIRVANA (A)

BABY FACE (I)

WALL

CARSON (A)

T-Bar I

Chair #2

Grand Chalet

GULL CANYON (A)

THE FACE (A)

SLALOM (A)

SKI AREA BOUNDARY

Snowmaking Area

Chair #5

Chair #1

SKI AREA BOUNDARY

Night Skiing

Ticket Office

PARKING

LEGEND
(N) Novice Runs
(I) Intermediate Runs
(A) Advanced Runs

WINTER IN JUNE LAKE

JUNE MOUNTAIN SKI AREA   ROCKY ROCKWELL

WINTER IN JUNE LAKE

Winter in June Lake is tremendous. The beauty of the snow-capped peaks which surround the Alpine setting of the village with the convenience of the ski lifts and activities, make this a very popular winter resort. The lifts are situated about one mile west of June Lake Village.

Sierra Pacific Airlines serves June Mountain with several daily flights into the Mammoth Lakes Airport, just a few miles south of June Lake. Bus services and car rentals are obtainable at the airport. Flights leave daily from Los Angeles, Burbank, San Jose and Fresno. Highway 395 is open except during storms. Greyhound buses run daily from many points.

Due to the low relative humidity and temperatures of the eastern Sierra, some of the finest skiing conditions exist on June Mountain. There are many runs and slopes for skiiers from the novice to the expert.

At the top of Chair Lift #1, outside the Grand Chalet is Peanutville — a supervised, instructional and snow play area for the young set. There are four chair lifts and one T-bar rising 2562 feet from the June Lake Loop road to the top of June Mountain. Ski lessons are available with the highly successful Head-Way Learn to Ski Lesson Course for both beginners and advanced skiiers. For more information on this write June Mountain Head-Way, P.O. Box 146, June Lake, Calif. 93529.

Two cross-country/nordic ski trails are in the area. Lessons are available for this unique skiing experience. The June Mountain Racing Team has been organized for skiers of all ages who are interested in serious competition with NASTAR and the Far West Ski Association Competition Program.

73

WINTER IN ROCK CREEK

With the yellowing of the aspens and the migration of the warblers go the RV's and the fishermen. As the temperature drops, only the crackling ice in Little Lakes Valley disturb the silence. Snowflake by snowflake the scars of summer are covered. Rock Creek Winter Lodge offers an extensive program that has safe and convenient access to this winter wonderland where snow transforms the ordinary into magnificence.

From Hwy. 395 westward the first six miles of the Rock Creek Canyon Road are plowed by the U.S. Forest Service. There are several miles of groomed trails adjacent to the parking facilities. Radiating from this area is an extensive network of marked and semi-maintained trails that lead to Morgan Pass and beyond.

Two miles over the snow at 9300', Rock Creek Winter Lodge presents a unique winter wilderness experience. Snow-cat rides are available from the parking area to the resort. Fourteen rustic cabins along with a dining room and central hall provide possible enjoyment of this winter environment with comfort. Home-cooked meals are the pride of the Lodge.

Their program includes natural history tours, ski mountaineering, snow-shoeing, cross-country ski rentals and instruction, base camps within the Rock Creek drainage, and guided crossings over the Bishop, Mono and Muir passes opening the realm of Trans-Sierra tours that appeal to a range of skiing abilities. Evening entertainment is by slide program or movie. Guests are encouraged to participate by bringing their own 35 mm slides or musical instruments.

74

ROCK CREEK CROSS-COUNTRY SKIING   MARK WILLIAMS

WINTER SAFETY

For your winter visit to the ski slopes and backcountry cross-country Nordic skiing, Mark Williams of the Rock Creek Winter Lodge offers some advice.

"Observing simple rules during the winter insures personal safety with increased enjoyment of the activity you are engaged in. Hypothermia — subnormal body temperature — is the number one killer of winter recreationists. The lowering of the internal body heat leads to mental and physical collapse. Initial symptoms are uncontrollable fits of shivering, vague slow speech, immobile or fumbling hands. Advanced stages involve memory lapse, incoherent frequent stumbling, exhaustion and drowsiness.

Use a layered clothing method, which can be adjusted to the prevailing conditions. Wool, which retains most of its insulating value when wet, is still the best choice for winter wear. Some of the new synthetics, such as polarguard, fiber-fill, and thinsulate also work well. A loose fitting windproof outer shell of nylon or Gore-tex fabrics is essential. For more information read the U.S.F.S. pamphlet on hypothermia.

Other winter hazards are:

Frostbite which is the result of unprotected skin to subfreezing temperatures. Your feet and toes are usually the areas affected most. Wear boots that are not tight as well as one pair of wool socks and, carry extras.

Dehydration is the loss of water by strenuous activity. To avoid this, drink frequently to quench your thirst. For winter snow travel, a canteen of something hot like soup, tea, or coffee is good.

Before leaving on any expedition, check with the Ranger Station at Bishop or Mammoth Lakes of avalanche alert and to pick up free information to help plan a safe winter trip. Snow storms arrive suddenly, bringing harsh winds, cold, and white out. Take emergency gear into the backcountry necessary to lay over until the weather clears. Notify a responsible person of your **75** planned route and expected time of return. "

THE SIERRA ENVIRONMENT

The east slope of the Sierra is so abrupt between the floor of Owens Valley and the Sierra crest adjacent to it, that climatic conditions are not as consistent with changes in elevations as on the west. Here will be found a general intermingling of both plant and animal life except at extreme elevations. All life, as well as climatic conditions, are compressed into such a limited space definite separations are seldom found.

Life Zones are a reflection of weather belts where there is a reasonable consistancy of certain shrubs and trees suitable to the shelter and food supply for its wildlife. Soil conditions, moisture, exposure to sunlight, and season of the year produce many variations. Elevation alone, although significant, is not a sole definitive determinent.

Most regions have a fairly stable weather situation developing from elevation and latitude. The Sierra region follows this weather and life zone pattern only as it relates to southern or northern areas. A venture into the Sierra either east or west produces dramatic changes in weather, plant life, and the wildlife. Add to this the changing conditions of soil, moisture, and sunny exposure, the visitor could cross in the space of a few days or hours, as many physical life zones as if traveling several thousand miles from the southwestern Sonora desert to the northern Canadian arctic.

In the Upper Sonoran Zone (from 6000' to 7500') the pinyon pine and Sierra juniper are found. The Jeffrey pine forest is in the Transition Zone (7500' to 8000'). Lodgepole pine, red fir and white fir are found in the Canadian Zone (8000' to 9000'). From 9000' to timberline, about 11,000', is the Hudsonian Zone where the western white pine, mountain hemlock, lodgepole pine and whitebark pine are found. Above 11,000' in the barren slopes with a few scattered dwarf trees and plants, is the Alpine Zone.

EASTERN SIERRA CONE-BEARING TREES

The PINYON PINE occupied a special place in the life habits of the desert Indians. The profusion of large, oily, nuts from their cones ripening in the fall determined the coming and going of early people as they harvested the winter food. Pinyon nuts were a basic part of their trading goods with other tribes. Groves, and in places, forests of pinyon pines present a rolling gray-green carpet over the dry, east Sierra foothills. They are found in small, open plateaus scattered in-between low ridges with little or no competition from other trees.

They usually are 8' to 25' high; 12" to 15" in diameter. Their cones grow to 3" and are almost round. Needles are short, one to a bundle— the only pine with a single needle.

The WHITE FIR grows tall, from 140' to 180' with its diamete 3½' to 6'. It is a very massive tree, with the lower third clear of brar ches. They can be found in the Transition and Canadian Zones. Th cones stand erect on the outer tips of limbs near the top of the tree Bark is 4" to 6½" thick, silvery on young trees, ash-gray to dee brownsih-yellow beneath. Young stems have resin blisters. Needl are single, 1" to 3" long—the longest of any fir. They stand out from branches with a twist at its base. They are green with whitish ting Some trees range from 275 to 400 years old.

The RED FIR is found usually in the Canadian zone. They grow from 125' to 175' tall many with broken crowns. They are 1½' to 5½' in diameter but there are trees 20" to 30" in diameter averaging 225 to 375 years old. The bark is 2" to 5" thick, deeply fissured and divided by short, diagonal ridges. The outer scales are dark red and the inner segments are bright red. The surface is rough. Cones stand erect near the tips of branches. They range from 5" to 8" long and 3" to 3½" in diameter–purplish, with edges of brown. The needles are ¼" to 1¼" long, four-sided, rounded on top. They are attached directly to the stem. Limbs form heavy sprays in whorl formations.

The LODGEPOLE PINE with its twisted trunks are often lightning scarred. They grow to the height of 30' to 80' and are usually 1' to 2½' in diameter. Their bark is very thin, light gray and yellowish-brown in color and very scaly. They grow to be from 100 to 175 years old. The cones are numerous, pitch-free, small, and 1¼" to 2½" long and 1" to 2" in diameter. Needles are two in a bundle, about 1" to 2¼" long and yellowish-green, often twisted. Indians and pioneers used the long straight trunks for teepees and cabins. With such thin bark, they were easy to peel.

The beautiful MOUNTAIN HEMLOCK has limbs that grow close to the ground. They can be found from 7700' to timberline in shaded north slopes or cold canyons. There are a number at Minaret Vista, and in the Mammoth Lakes Basin area. They reach 25' to 100' in height and 1' to 3½' in diameter. Older trees, those about 200 years old, are 50' in height amd 18" to 20" in diameter. The bark of young trees is thin and silvery; mature trees anout 1½" thick, and reddish-brown; deeply ridged and furrowed. Cones are abundant at the top of the trees, 1" to 4" long and ½" to 1½" in diameter. The small, less-than-an-inch long needles grow spirally around branches, and appear thicker on the upper side.

The SIERRA JUNIPER is a tough and rugged tree, with heavy twisted trunks; 10' to 30' average in height and 3' to 6' in diameter. Their bark is 2½" to 5" thick; reddish-brown with long, fibrous edges of soft bark which is easily stripped from the trunks. Their small cones are more like berries, divided into three sections covered with a whitish bloom with a very pungent odor. The needles are very short–¼" long and scalelike, overlapping in clusters of three (similar to the incense cedar) and gray-green in color. On the Valentine Lake Trail are a few stands of tall, imposing junipers. They are found on rocky hillsides from the Canadian to Hudsonian zones. Some older trees reach ages from 500 to 1500 years.

77

The LIMBER PINE, at maturity, reaches up to 50'to 60' with diameters to 3' to 4'. Their thick, dark brown bark and long, spreading arms make a great photographic contrast against gray rocks and towering skylines. Its twisted, scraggly forms are seen all along the slopes in the Hudsonian Zone near timberline. Its limber quality is very flexible in withstanding severe storms. Their cones are from 3½" to 10" long. Needles are in groups of five, 1" to 1¼" long.

The WHITEBACK PINE grows in sheltered areas to 15' to 40' high and 15" to 30" in diameter. However, on open ridges they grow in a sprawling, prostrate, shrublike manner surviving the bitter winds and many months covered with snow. They are found in the Hudsonian Zone to timberline. Their thick bark is gray on mature trunks blending to whitish on smooth, outer limbs. The cones are 1¼" to 3½" long, and from 1" to 2" in diameter, oval-shaped, very pitchy with thick scales, and purplish in color. Their needles are five in a bundle and up to ½" long, dark yellow-green, and thickly clustered near the ends of branches. It takes a long time for the tree to grow due to a short season, some only about a half inch per year.

BROADLEAVED TREES AND SHRUBS

The gay, fluttering QUAKING ASPEN are water lovers and can be found in groves along streams between 6000' to 10,000' elevation. Their slim trunks grow to a height of 20' to 40'. The bark often indicates the scratch marks of passing animals or thoughtless humans. Their light green leaves, undercoated with silvery-white waver in the slightest breeze. In the autumn they come into their own special glory when they present their great show in the high mountains when the graceful groups turn to gold, orange, and yellow masses of color. They are found up in McGee Creek, around Convict Lake, Hilton Creek, Lundy Creek, LeeVining Canyon and Rock Creek.

78

The MANZANITA ("Little apple" in Spanish) is an evergreen varying in height from 5" to 6" to several feet, depending on species and locality. It has very hardwood limbs that grow in twisted, distorted patterns. Its deep, red limbs are contrasted by its gray-green leaves, and white urn-shaped flowers. The green and reddish berries resemble small apples and were used by the pioneers to make jelly.

The WILLOW FAMILY loves water. They are found in both bush and tree forms that grow along streams from the foothills to the highest meadows. The slender, limber branches bearing narrow pale-green leaves shade the trout nearby and make nesting shelter for birds.

The ALPINE WILLOW grows beyond the last whitebark pine in moist snow-fed tundra sending forth its limbs in matted patterns just under the surface. It presents its blooms with tiny, 2" tall catkins with a few narrow dark green leaves to protect and encourage its efforts of survival in such a difficult environment.

DEER BRUSH, or Ceanothus, or "Wild Lilac" has a delicate, pyramidal spiked white or blue flower. It is a member of the Buckhorn family, and is found on hillsides creating dense coverage for birds and small animals. It blooms in the spring. The leaves are sticky and dark green. The bush grows up to five feet tall.

Other species of Ceanothus are the SIERRA SNOWBRUSH with a white, sweet-smelling flower found from 5000' to 10,000'. The BUCK BRUSH with similar blossoms have smaller leaves than the Deer Brush. This species also gives shelter and provides nest sites for birds. The bark and roots were used in earlier times for home remedies.

WILD ROSE is very common and found in meadows from 6000' to 8000'. It is a ragged, scraggly shrub with lovely pink blossoms in the early summer. The rich perfume attracts many butterflies and bees. By fall the fruit becomes red berries and the leaves turn from a deep green to a rich reddish-brown.

The LABRADOR TEA belongs to the Heath Family. It is a low bush that grows in high elevations, found in boggy places near streams and lakes. The umbrel cluster of small white flowers has a bitter odor when blooming. Tea was made from the green leaves which thickly coat the stem of the plant. It was good for rheumatism. (It is shown on the inside front cover.)

FLOWERS

During the comparitively short growing season from the last snowfall in the late spring to the first snowfall of winter, flowers of many varieties present themselves in breathless haste to complete their life-cycle. There are hundreds of beautiful species growing among rocky ledges, in lush meadows, on sandy slopes, or along streams and in open as well as sheltered areas. Most of the flowers that are prevelent on the east side of the Sierra are found on the west side as well. The most hearty mountaineers that grow among the high altitude rocks are the red and white heather and the sky-blue polemonium. They persevere in such unlikely places as up to 12,000' against the granite skyline ridges.

The COLUMBINE, loved by hummingbirds for their nectar in the long flower spurs, belong to the Buttercup family. Blossoms are found to be red, yellow or white. Stems are from 1' to 3' high and slender. They are seen at high elevations to timberline where the blue High Mountain Columbine grows.

The MARSH MARIGOLD belongs to the Buttercup family. The flowers are white with stems erect, from 4" to 12", without leaves. They enjoy moist places at high elevation. Leaves are up to 4" wide. (shown on inside back cover)

80

The MONKEY FLOWER belongs to the Figwort family. Has a brilliant yellow flower with brown spots of about one inch across. The stems are fragile and the leaves very delicate. They like running water and grow in elevations up to 10,000'. Another variety is the spectacular SCARLET MIMULUS (shown on inside front cover). Has a velvet texture and is extremely popular with hummingbirds. The MIMULUS LEWISII, named after Meriweather Lewis, is one of the most beautiful of all. It also enjoys streamsides and is found in a wide range of elevations. (shown on inside back cover)

The INDIAN PAINT BRUSH is another member of the Figwort family. Flowers are red, 1 to 1½" long, clustered in dense terminal spikes. They are quite common and found in moist meadows up to 10,000'. Closely related to the OWL'S CLOVER (both seen on inside back cover). This pink-purplish flower grows in lower elevations, stands erect from 6" to 12" high. The leaves are parted into many narrow segments.

BLEEDING HEART is a member of the Fumitory family. Their rose-purple heart-shaped flowers are clustered near the end of long, naked stems. Leaves with many lobes are from creeping rootstalks. Plants are usually from 10" to 15" high. They are found in shaded wooded areas in high to moderate elevations. (shown on inside back cover)

The BLUE GENTIAN can be seen in meadows from 7000' to 10,000'. The leaves are short and narrow. Stems can bear a single, erect tubular, terminal flower. Other species such as the tiny white alpine gentian is found in higher elevations while at lower elevations is a gentian with fringed edges to the petals.

The DOUGLAS PHLOX is a member of the Gilia family, found on dry-gravelled slopes from 7500' to timberline. The small, lavender flower blooms all at once at the end of short branches. The stems are very leafy forming stiff mats with densely crowded leaves.

The SCARLET GILIA is the most spectacular of the Gilia family with its tube-shaped flower. They grow in loose, gravelly soil at moderate elevations. They are sometimes mistaken for the SCARLET PENSTEMON as both flowers are tall with red blossoms. The leaves are divided into long, narrow sections formed at the base of the plant. (shown on inside front cover)

81

The WILD GERANIUM has pink to white blossoms with petals of deep red veins. The stems stand erect up to 2' high. The leaves are from 2" to 4" wide, rounded and divided into five to seven segments. The plant is very popular, commonly found in meadows or along shaded streams from up to 9000'. (shown on inside front cover)

The WHITE and RED HEATHER belong to the Heath family. They grow low in dense mats. The white heather (cassiope — one of John Muir's favorites) has a bell-shaped flower while the blossoms of the red heather is similar to the alpine laurel, also a member of the Heath family. The stem of the red heather has tiny, dark green leaves like pine needles.

The LEOPARD LILY or Tiger Lily grow in wet meadows and alongside streams in moderate elevations. Their leaves are whorled and the blossoms are spotted, hence the reference to the spotted animals. They are commonly found in orange-yellow with purple ends in July and August. They like wet banks and are one of the more outstanding varieties of the entire lily family (shown on inside back cover). A LITTLE LEOPARD LILY is found in boggy places in elevations up to 10,000' and are also known for thier sweet, delicate scent.

The CORN LILY grows tall up to 5' high resembling cornstalks. The flowers are dull white, clustered in tassel-like spears. The leaves are large and form dense patches in wet meadows. Indians used this plant for many remedies. It has been mistaken for "skunk cabbage" in the early spring when it first begins to grow.

Another member of the Lily family is the MARIPOSA LILY with
their creamy-white petals and dark centers. A cup-shaped flower
found in dry, open slopes and flat areas from 6500' to 8000'. The
single, erect and stiff stem grow to about a foot in height. Blooms
from May to July. Mariposa is the Spanish name for butterfly. Indians liked to eat the roasted bulbs.

The Wild SWAMP ONION is a member of the Lily family. They
are very common, found in wet meadows from 5000' to 9000'. The
plant has strong onion or garlic odor as signified by its Latin name
Allium. The bulbs are used by mountaineers for food and flavoring.
The rose-purple flower is in umbrella-like heads with stout, leafless
stems about 2' to 3' high. The leaves are long and grass-like.

The COW PARSNIP belongs to the Parsley family. Its white
flower with innumerable heads form an umbrella-like cluster, about
to 10" wide. The leaves are in groups of three, deeply lobed and
othed from 3" to 12" across. The stems are coarse and hollow.
they like damp meadows and streamsides in elevations up to 8000'.

83

LUPINE belongs to the Pea family. Flowers are blue or pink, crowded together, all whoring around the upper part of the stem. They are common in meadows and various species are found throughout the Sierra. Some grow on dry slopes, other prefer shade, but all are long blooming. (shown on inside front cover)

The CALIFORNIA INDIAN PINK, a Pink family member also called Catchfly or Campion. The name "pink" refers not only to the color but to the pinking of the petals. Found in brush or open wooded areas in moderate elevations. The brilliant tiny scarlet blossoms with deep cleft petals are seen from spring to fall. Leaves are from 1" to 3" long, stems about a foot high. (shown on inside front cover)

The THISTLE POPPY is known for its prickly stems and beauti white flower with yellow centers. As in all flowers of the poppy far ly, the petals are very delicate. The stems grow up to 3' and can seen from 5000' to 8500' along the road.

JEFFREY SHOOTING STAR is a member of the Primrose fam The rose-pink or lavender blossoms are long with a yellow base a distinct purple bank, resembling a cyclamen. Stems are naked, a grows up to 18" high bearing a cluster of five to ten flowers. T leaves are yellowish-green and long shooting up from the base of plant. They grow in wet meadows or other moist places up to 10,0(

The SIERRA PRIMROSE grows along granite boulders above timberline, blooming in July soon after the snow melts. The rose-purple blossoms stand on erect stems above basal leaves. It is a tiny plant about 5" high bearing an umbrel of five to ten flowers. Leaves are spoon-shaped and scalloped. (shown on inside back cover) The EVENING PRIMROSE is much taller, has a yellow flower, is found along streams and in sandy meadows up to 8000'.

Another member of the Purslane family is the PUSSY PAWS which grows close to the ground and spreads its dark green leaves out flat. The rose colored flower in a dense cluster is at the end of an erect stem. The stems have few leaves and are about 4" to 10" long. They are found in dry, open areas above 8000'.

MINERS LETTUCE is a tiny little flower belonging to the Purslane family. The dainty, succulent basal leaves and stems were eaten by Indians and miners as greens. The flower lives in shady spots. The blossoms are a pinky-white with stems growing up to one foot high, bare except for a pair of united leaves just below the flowers.

SNEEZEWEED is a member of the Sunflower family. They are very common in meadows and along streams at moderate elevations. The yellow rays droop from the yellow disks with stems branching from 2" to 4" high. The green leaves are about 4" to 10" long. (shown on inside front cover)

FERNS

Ferns are not as frequently seen on the eastern slopes and meadows of the Sierra due to the lack of moisture and rich soil. They are found up Rock Creek, LeeVining Canyon, along the Tioga Road, and Mono Pass. Ferns differ from flowering plants and cone-bearing trees as they produce spores, not flowers or seeds. With the roots, stems, and leaves water minerals and food is conducted throughout the plant. The roots absorb the water and minerals from the soil. Some roots have to grow deep to gain the necessary moisture in dryer canyons.

LITTLE GRAPE FERN (Botryschium simplex): a slender plant from 2" to 5" high. Its habitat is among grasses and sedges in alpine meadows above 10,000'. It is widespread throughout the world but often overlooked due to its size as it is seldom taller than the grasses around it. This perennial plant grows from a fibrous root, usually bearing one leaf per year.

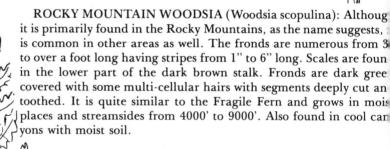

ROCKY MOUNTAIN WOODSIA (Woodsia scopulina): Althoug it is primarily found in the Rocky Mountains, as the name suggests, is common in other areas as well. The fronds are numerous from 3 to over a foot long having stripes from 1" to 6" long. Scales are foun in the lower part of the dark brown stalk. Fronds are dark gree covered with some multi-cellular hairs with segments deeply cut an toothed. It is quite similar to the Fragile Fern and grows in moi: places and streamsides from 4000' to 9000'. Also found in cool car yons with moist soil.

BREWERS CLIFF BRAKE (Pellaea breweri): This delicate fern enjoys high elevations growing prostrate under rocky ledges and straight up when in open meadows. The plants grow up to 9" with

86 fronds in clumps. It is also referred to as the Sierra Cliff Brake. They have two or three leaflets growing together on the main stalk opposite each other.

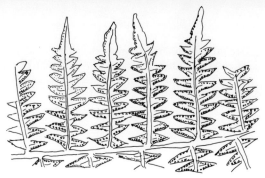

BRAKE FERN (Pteridium aquilinum): One of the most common ferns found in wooded areas or open meadows. It is a coarse, acid-loving fern. They become a dense stand when growing in moist meadows. A single frond is from 2' to 4' high and grows each year from the end of the branch of the long black stem. The underground stem was used for making baskets and textiles by the California Indians. The young tender fronds were eaten by the Indians both raw and cooked.

FIVE FINGER FERN (Adiantum pedatum): Also referred to as the American Maiden Hair not to be confused with the Common Maiden Hair. This plant has slender rootstocks, long fronds forked at the tip of the stripe on strong branches. The stripes are polished, purplish, about 1' to 2' high. The blades are rounded in outline being 8" to 18" wide. It is a common fern found from 3000' to 10,000'. A very distinguished plant, graceful and delicate with the leaf stalks black or brown and sometimes shiny. They grow in moist places protected from the direct sun.

PARSLEY FERN (Cryptogramma crispa): American Rock Fern is another name for this plant found at elevations 5000' to 10,000' in cracks of granite. They have two different fronds: the sterile frond is 2" to 8" long with blades 1" to 5" wide. The small sterile fronds are clustered and the branches have a narrow wing with flat leaflets down the stalk. The fertile fronds are taller with no wings on the stalk.

87

BIRDS

STELLER'S JAY: Large, flashy blue color. Noisy, raucous voice and bold, saucy habits. Eats insects, nuts and grain. Lively companion in camp or along the trail. Large feathered crest on head that is dark, extending to a blue-black on shoulders and wings. Light blue-gray on underparts. Larger than a robin.

AMERICAN DIPPER (Water Ouzel): Perches on rocks in midstream and bobs up and down when standing. Dives under water for food  and propels himself with wings when submerged. They eat water insects and larvae. Nests are at waterline or behind the spray of waterfalls. Slate-gray, shading to dark on wings and sides of head. Very stubby tail, large strong legs with sharp clawed feet for the slippery rocks. Sings loudly amid the roaring stream enjoying snow and cold and rain as much as a sunny day.

 CHICKADEE (Mountain Chickadee or Short-tailed Mountain Chickadee): Has a persistent, identifying call of "chick-a-dee" or plaintive "ee-chee-chee" heard in the high country. Found on the tip-top twig of the tallest tree. Somewhat smaller than a sparrow. Top of head and throat dark, has white line over eye, cheeks and breast are also white.

JUNCO (Oregon, Thurber's or Sierra Junco): Has quite dark "cape" over head and shoulders; underside is white. Light brown on shoulders and back, center tail feathers black, outer ones white, legs and feet pink with a light-colored bill. Feeds on ground around base of trees, particularly mountain hemlock or white fir.

ROBIN: They return to the mountains in June. The red breast; black head and tail, gray back and yellow bill heralds spring. They eat worms and are found near mountain lakes and in meadows. They also feed on insects and berries.

BLUEBIRD (Mountain Bluebird): Seen in high country meadows, slightly larger than the sparrow. Feeds on insects from the ground and spends considerable time perched on top of rocks singing. Bright blue all over except for a lighter shade on underside. Females are usually a paler color.

WHITE-CROWNED SPARROW: Distinguished from other sparrows by black and white stripes on head with one white stripe running above bill through center of crown. Light grayish-brown on back, underparts light. Are seen near thickets in mountain meadows about 7500' to 9000'. Nests on low willow branches, eats insects in summer and seed sprouts in winter. Has a melodious, plaintive song.

WESTERN TANAGER: Their flight in and out of sunlight and shadow is a thing of startling beauty. Vivid scarlet head, upper back and tail dark, wings black with yellow bars, rest of body a striking yellow. Females are drab-green above and yellowish underparts. Their movements are slow and deliberate, building nests towards the ends of branches in the forest from 7000' to 9000'.

CLARK'S NUTCRACKER: This is a high country bird usually seen at timberline. Has a noisy cry, quite companionable to people. Pale gray body with dark wings, dark center on tail, outer edge of tail feathers and rest of wings in white. Size and habits similar to the Steller's Jay. They enjoy seeds from the Jeffrey and pinyon pine during the winter which they have stored in the fall. All summer they store whitebark pine seeds and in the early spring have food until the new crop of cones are ripe.

ROSY FINCH (Sierra Nevada Rosy Finch): Friendly companion of the high mountain climber. Seen in flocks feeding on snow fields or surface of glaciers. Nests in rocky cliffs along wind-swept ridges above timberline. Bright rosy hue on breast, rump, wings and shoulders. About the size of a sparrow. CASSIN'S PURPLE FINCH lives in lower elevations from 8000' tp 9000'. They forage for buds, insects and seeds. Their size similar to sparrow, rose-red on head with the back, neck, wings and tail brown. Rump, throat and breast a pale rose. Females are brown streaked with gray.

ANIMALS

The forested slopes and lush meadows of the Sierra provide a great variety of shelter and food for many kinds of animals, large and small. Here the land, its coverage of trees, shrubs, and grass, plus the moderate summer climate make up an ideal home for them.

Most birds, as well as some of the larger animals such as deer, move down into the foothills below snowline where the winter is less severe. The bear and the marmot prefer to sleep in sheltered caves through the long winter. They store up fat to last them through the hibernation period lasting usually from the middle of December to the middle of April. The chickaree and the cony build special nests in sheltered places and store up enough food to last throughout the winter.

The DEER and the SIERRA NEVADA BLACK BEAR are the two largest and most common animals. Deer depend largely upon leaves of certain brush and trees for food. Each spring they migrate back up the canyons—the buck with short, if any antlers, the does, heavy with fawns, on their way to their summer mountain home. The young black bear are born in the late winter while the mother is in hibernation. Sometimes they are several weeks old when the mother rouses from her sleep. She usually produces offsprings in pairs every other year.

It is evident that the POCKET GOPHER has been around from the earth cores or mounds that run under the ground in long coils. These cores result from activity in winter when the gopher makes tunnels in the snow in search for food. They are tillers of the soil moving many tons of dirt and provide openings for water to penetrate the surface crust down to the tree roots.

The BELDING GROUND SQUIRREL, or "picket-pin" is found in the mountain meadows. Its nickname refers to his picket-like stature when on watch near the opening of his burrow. They sit straight up, so straight and stiff by their mounds, then scurry inside when they see danger. They are yellowish brown on the upper sides and a shade lighter underneath. They eat grass, herbs, seeds and hibernate most of the winter—from November to mid March.

CHIPMUNK

The ever-busy CHIPMUNK are found around trees and brush. They are very small, have stripes extending along the sides of their bodies on up across their necks to include the sides of their face. They have a very sharp pointed nose. The GOLDEN-MANTLE GROUND SQUIRREL looks much like an oversized, well-fed chipmunk for which he is often mistaken. His personality is as colorful with his yellow-gold or copperish mantle. The black and white stripes on his sides do not extend to the face as on chipmunks.

CHICKAREE

The SIERRA CHICKAREE are seen from 7500' to timberline. They are heard wherever there are groves of trees and also referred to as the pine squirrel or the Douglas squirrel. They are about the size of a rat, dark brown with buff undersides.

MARMOT

In the highest meadows and slopes adjacent to the skyline crags is found the SOUTHERN SIERRA MARMOT, the largest of the squirrel family. They are vegetarians feeding in the meadows either to get over the long winter or to fatten up for the one to come. They have brownish-gray backs ticked with white, and are buff or yellowish-brown on the undersides. They like to bask in the sun on top of boulders and can be seen along the trail.

The CONY, or pika, a small, pale gray rodent the size of a small bush rabbit, seldom leaves his rocky home except when venturing a few yards into a meadow to feed or cut grass to store in his hay barn for winter. He lives in his burrow under sheltered rocks, tucked away from severe winter cold.

CONEY

92

SHASTA BEAVER were transplanted from Modoc County to Robinson Creek, up McGee Creek and Mill Creek above Lundy Lake. They are powerful and one of the largest rodents in North America. They have a flat tail, short inconspicuous ears on a squarish head, brown above, somewhat lighter in underparts. They enjoy bark, twigs, and wood from the willow, cottonwood, and especially aspen trees.

The YELLOW-HAIRED PORCUPINE is seldom seen but often noted for the girdle marks found on young fir trees. When the boughs or bark are chewed off at the top, it is usually the work of a porcupine. The height above ground is a fair clue as to the depth of the snow when it happened. Known for his quill-covered body, they are unaggressive and good-natured creatures. They shuffle clumsily and can swim as well as climb trees.

The SIERRA PINE MARTEN, resembling a large weasel, is extremely shy, nocturnal in habit and, therefore, seldom seen. The conies, squirrels and chickarees know him all too well as they are his favorite food. Living in rocky crevices at 7000' to 11,000' in the summer, the pine marten stays in trees during the winter. **93**

INDEX

IN APPRECIATION. . .

We would like to extend our thanks to those who have given their time and assistance in checking data, maps, and providing special photographs and other interpretive materials making this book as accurate, up-to-date, and useful as possible.

Wymond Eckhardt, NPS, Devils Postpile

Pam Gardner, Inyo National Forest, Bishop

Walt Hoffman, NPS, Devils Postpile

Tom Johnston, Mammoth Mountain

Patty Novak, Inyo National Forest, Mammoth Lakes

Rocky Rockwell, Eastern Sierra Interpretive Association

Joan Schultz, June Lake Chamber of Commerce

Mark Williams, Rock Creek Winter Lodge

Photographic credit for Front Cover and Title Pages: Rocky Rockwell

OTHER GUIDES BY LEW & GINNY CLARK

HIGH MOUNTAINS & DEEP VALLEYS, The Gold Bonanza Days
$6.95

The first book of its kind about the Basin and Range Country covering Death Valley, Ghost Towns from Calico to Virginia City, Owens Valley, Ancient Bristlecone Pine Forest and Eastern Approaches to the Sierra with colorful maps, sketches, photographs, wildlife notes, services available, camping notes, and travel conditions.

JOHN MUIR TRAIL COUNTRY $5.95

A profusely illustrated guide with many 4-color maps, trail profiles, photographs of the Sierra Nevada between the lower Kern River Country on the south to the Emigrant Basin Country on the north. In great detail the Clarks describe trails to explore, lakes to fish, peaks to climb and what to see along the famous John Muir Trail. Includes the western forest trails in the Sierra Wilderness areas from Sequoia to Yosemite National Parks.

YOSEMITE TRAILS $5.95

A complete guide to all the trails in Yosemite National Park with maps—some five color USGS topographic—trail notes, profile charts, showing elevations and mileages between important points. Wildlife notes, forest cover, geology and identification charts of trees and flowers. Many photographs and sketches. Special winter section with ski trails.

SIERRA WILDFLOWER PRINT-POSTALS Packet of twelve $2.00

These beautiful, very popular floral photographic prints are in full color. Twelve different favorite Sierra flowers for you to treasure or send to a friend. In plastic packet.

MT. WHITNEY TRAILS (Sequoia National Park) $1.25
KINGS RIVER COUNTRY (Kings Canyon National Park) $1.25

Large, handy fold-up guides in plastic pouch. Updated, five-color USGS topographic maps with descriptive east and west entries with trail notes. Full-color photographs and covers. Trail profiles and mountaineering notes. Better than a topo!